eat.shop london 2nd edition

an encapsulated view of the most interesting, inspired and authentic
locally owned eating and shopping establishments in london, england

researched, photographed and written by caroline lonce
cabazon books : 2010

table of contents

eat

shop

caroline's notes on london

When I think about the journey of discovery I have made while working on this second *eat.shop london* edition, I feel as though I have opened up another treasure box full of glittering, intriguing playthings. London is my city, my old friend, whom I have seen dressed up and down, in blue skies and grey. With this book I discovered a new facet to our friendship, a new wardrobe, if you will, and my love for this sprawling, squiggling city, that laughs in the face of a grid system, has renewed itself once again.

Eating and shopping are always fun, but London also thrills me culturally, with unparalleled theatre, art and music springing up, like weeds in cracked pavements, wherever there is space to play. There are new tribes emerging all the time, each bringing their own dish to the cultural table, so don't miss out on these while you're here.

Central London is surprisingly compact with some neighbourhoods only a few streets wide, making for good walking. I highly suggest getting the *A-Z London Mini Street Atlas* in paperback for your back pocket, and download the bus maps pdfs at www.tfl.gov.uk and familiarise yourself with those (you can use their website to help you plan a route, too).

For the fearless, there are now thousands of bikes in central London available to hire cheaply (www. tfl.gov.uk/roadusers/cycling/14808.aspx). As a hardened London cyclist, I do urge you to follow these maxims: assume that every vehicle is, whether consciously or subconsciously, trying to kill you. Get off and walk across junctions you don't understand. Keep well away from bendy buses and anything with wheels bigger than a car. Wear bright clothing. Smile You'll be fine. And if riding isn't your thing, but walking is, here are a couple of my favorite day strolls:

1 > *The South Bank Stroll*: Go from Jubilee Gardens (Waterloo) to the Design Museum (Bermondsey), wiggling back to the river whenever you are forced away.

2 > *The Grand Union Canal*: From Limehouse Station on the DLR to the Angel, or from the Angel (Muriel street) to Camden and Regent's Park, then away from the Canal to Primrose Hill.

3 > *The Views*: Start at Primrose Hill, then wander through Camden and meander up to Parliament Hill, then hop on the train at Hampstead Heath to go straight round to Richmond for the Richmond hill spectacular.

And a couple more ideas beyond eating and shopping: The Chelsea Physic Garden is a hidden treasure (www.chelseaphysicgarden.co.uk), The London Wetland Centre is an urban paradise if you like feathered friends (www.wwt.org.uk/london) and Kew Gardens is a year-round stunner with the nearby *Maids of Honour Tearoom* beckoning for afters (www.kew.org).

about eat.shop

• All of the businesses featured in this book are locally owned. In deciding which businesses to feature, that's the number one criteria. We also tend to veer away from chains or business "groups" where there are more than four outlets. Then we look for businesses that strike us as utterly authentic and uniquely conceived, whether they be new or old, chic or funky. And if you were wondering, businesses don't pay to be featured—that's not our style.

• A note about our maps. They are stylized, meaning they don't show every street. In a city like London where there zillions of little streets or streets change names, it's imperative you carry a more detailed map like an A - Z Map for London. We also have an online map with the indicators of the businesses noted > map.eatshopguides.com/lon2. And a little note about exploring a city. The businesses we feature are mainly in neighborhoods within the urban core (excepting Richmond and Hampstead in this edition). Each of these 'hoods (and others that we don't cover) have scads of great stores and restaurants other than the ones listed in this book, so give yourself time to explore.

• Because the author of this book is a Brit, you'll note that spellings are British English instead of American English. If this looks a bit strange to you, we suggest you sit down with and have a pint or two of Black Sheep Ale, and then it will look fine.

• This is important: make sure to double check the hours of the business before you go, as many places change their hours seasonally.

• The pictures and descriptions for each business are meant to give you a feel for a place, and are the items that the author were drawn to. Please don't take the business to task if what you see or read is no longer available.

• Small local businesses have always had to work their behinds off to keep their heads above water. During these rough economic times, sadly some won't make it. Does this mean the book is no longer valid? No way! The more you use this book and visit these businesses, the better chance they have to thrive.

• Please support the indie bookstores in London. To find these bookstores, use this great source: http://bit.ly/cyLfDz

• There are three ranges of prices noted for restaurants, $ = cheap, $$ = medium, $$$ = expensive

previous edition businesses

If you own the prevous edition of *eat.shop london*, make sure to keep it. Think of each edition as part of an overall "volume" of books, as all of the businesses not featured in this new edition are still fantastic. The reason earlier edition businesses aren't in this book is because there are so many amazing businesses that deserve a chance to be featured!

eat

algerian coffee stores
andrew edmunds
barrafina
el vergel
eyre brothers
fika
flat white
frizzante
gastro
great queen street
green & red
green valley
jones dairy
la fromagerie
leila's shop
little georgia
locanda locatelli
makan café
marine ices
medcalf
ottolenghi
pellicci's
pinchito
raoul's
rochelle canteen
saki

spinach & agushi
sweet
tayyabs
teasmith
the cinnmon club
the elk in the woods
the golden hind
the roya oak
treacle
verde & co.
william curley
wright brothers

shop

albam
alfie's antique market
b store
b tailoring
bagman and robin
ben southgate
beyond the valley
caravan
comfort station
d.r. harris
divette
duke of uke
ella doran
equa
fred bare
g smith & sons
geo f. trumper
handmade & found
happie loves it
hurwundeki
international magic
joel & son
olive loves alfie
persephone books
queens
radio days

rellik
scarlet & violet
story
the african waistcoat co.
the old curiosity shop
twentytwentyone
unto this last

if a previous edition business does not appear on this list, it is either featured again in this edition, has closed or no longer meets our criteria or standards.

where to lay your weary head

there are many great places to stay in london, but here are a few favorites:

40 winks
109 mile end road e1 4uj (east london : stepney green)
020 7790 0259 / 40winks.org double from £130
notes: two guest bedrooms in a designer's stunning abode

town hall hotel & apartments
8 patriot square e2 9nf (east london : bethnel green)
020 7871 0460 / townhallhotel.com double from £150 one bedroom apt. from £250 restaurant: viajante
notes: spacious rooms, basement swimming pool

hoxton hotel
81 great eastern street ec2a 3hu (east london : shoreditch)
020 7550 1000 / hoxtonhotels.com double from £60 restaurant: hoxton grill
notes: upmarket at a low cost

the rookery hotel
12 peter's lane, cowcross street ec1m 6ds (the city : clerkenwell)
20 7336 0931 / rookeryhotel.com double from £220
notes: period charm

the zetter
st. john's square 86-88 clerkenwell road ec1m 5rj (the city : clerkenwell)
020 7324 4444 / thezetter.com double from £160 restaurant: bistro bruno loubet
notes: vintage modern style

the portobello hotel
22 stanley gardens w11 2ng (notting hill)
020 7727 2777 / portobellohotel.com double from £190
notes: small and charmingly offbeat

the pelham hotel
15 cromwell place sw7 2la (south kensington)
020 7589 8288 / pelhamhotel.co.uk double from £200 restaurant: bistro 15
notes: gorgeous town house hotel

anar persian kitchen

tranquil persian restaurant

349 portobello road w10 5sa. corner of bonchurch road
tube: ladbroke grove
020.8960.6555 www.anarpersiankitchen.co.uk
mon - thu noon - 11p fri - sat noon - 11.30p sun noon - 10p

opened in 2010. owner: amir-abbas moaven. chef: navid pasha
$-$$: all major credit cards accepted
lunch. dinner. full bar. reservations accepted

portobello > **e01**

Allow me to introduce my new love: Persian food, with its intriguing and tantalising flavour combinations. The romance began when my old friend Crispin introduced the note of dried lime into my kitchen symphony, and it has flourished since my discovery of the lovely *Anar Persian Kitchen*. The aromas here seduced me as I cycled by one day, and I returned to eat soon after. An excellent lunch which my Persian cuisine fire even higher so I went straight from lunch to *Books for Cooks* to buy some Persian cookbooks. There is no higher praise.

imbibe / devour:
dough (salty yoghurt drink)
abgoosht (lamb stew)
kashkeh bademjan (aubergine, walnuts, mint)
asheh reshteh (hearty broth with beans)
joojeh-bi-ostokhan (saffron chicken)
ghorme sabzi (lamb and herb-infused stew)
faloodeh (sorbet with frozen noodles,
  rose water and lime juice)

angels & gypsies

south london tapas with flair

29 - 33 camberwell church street se5 8tr. corner of kimpton street
rail: denmark hill or buses
020.7703.5984 www.churchstreethotel.com/restaurant.asp
mon - fri noon - 3.30p, 6 - 10.30p sat - sun noon - 4, 6 - 10.30p

opened in 2009. owner / chef: mel raido. owner: jose raido
$-$$: visa. mc
lunch. dinner. full bar. reservations accepted

camberwell > 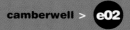 **e02**

When I told Daisy I was going to Camberwell to check out a restaurant foodies were buzzing about, she said, "Oh, I bet that's Mel's place. It's amazing," both were true. Mel, one of two brothers who have relaunched their family hotel and restaurant to a rapturous reception, is, it turns out, an actor as well as a fabulous chef: a polymath after my own heart, which, of course, makes me love *Angels & Gypsies* even more. The food, ranking among the very best of my delicious *eat.shop* journey, makes this place worth the trip every time.

imbibe / devour:
extensive wine list
pan-fried pumpkin with scotch bonnet pepper
fennel & chicory on the plancha
tuna tartare with avocado, pistachios &
  sea urchin caviar
angus sirloin with black beans & fried quail's egg
scottish clams with jamon, sherry & spring greens
seared rabbit fillet with chickpeas & wild garlic

asmara

family run, eritrean restaurant
386 coldharbour lane sw9 8lf. between atlantic and brixton roads
tube: brixton 020.7737.4144
mon - sun 5.30 - late

opened in 1994. owner / chef: hareghewein zerejohannes
$-$$: visa. mc
dinner. full bar. reservations accepted

brixton >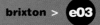

It's a strange experience eating Eritrean food alone when it's so obviously made for sharing. First come the enjera: light, slightly soured thickish pancakes, laid out on a platter; your dishes go on top and in you tuck, breaking off the bread, scooping, chatting and laughing. Or just eating and taking pictures in my case. When the next table got curious about the camera and struck up a conversation I felt pathetically grateful, instantly less of a Billy no-mates, and much more in the *Asmara* groove. Which is a very good groove, by the way.

imbibe / devour:
traditional coffee
castel beer
ajibo behmilti (spinach with homemade cheese)
kulwa (lamb in spiced butter)
derho (spiced chicken stew)
temtemo (spicy lentils)
spicy f'ul mesdemas (mashed fava beans)
ask the waiter "what's great this evening?"

bistrotheque

hidden restaurant and cocktail bar

23 - 27 wadeson street e2 9dr. between cambridge heath and mowlem
tube: bethnal green or rail: cambridge heath
020.8983.7900 www.bistrotheque.com
see website for hours

opened in 2004. owners: david waddington and pablo flack. chef: tom collins
$$-$$$: all major credit cards accepted
brunch. lunch. dinner. cabaret bar. reservations recommended

bethnal green > **e04**

Pablo, David and Tom are a brilliant team who, since the first edition of this book came out in '08, have taken *Bistrotheque* from strength to strength. This spot tucked away in an East London warehouse has been a hit, but the team didn't rest on their laurels and launched a couple of hugely successful pop-up resturants in unlikely places (the Royal Academy and most recently on the roof in the middle of the Olympic site). Always marrying mischievous theatricality with fine dining like no one else, if this threesome were marooned on a desert island, we'd all be rowing their to join the party.

imbibe / devour:
dark & stormy cocktail
espresso martini
confit tomato & samphire terrine with basil purée
sardine fillets, capers, sultanas & pine nuts
roast sea bass, heirloom tomatoes & aubergine
roast chicken, garlic & wild rocket
honey & thyme roast peaches & mascarpone
strawberry & elderflower cheesecake

15

bocca di lupo

the mouth of italy in the heart of soho

12 archer street w1d 7bb. between rupert and great windmill streets
tube: piccadilly circus
020.7734.2223 www.boccadilupo.com
mon - sat 12.30 - 3p, 5.30 - midnight sun noon - 4p

opened in 2008. owner / chef: jacob kennedy. owner: victor hugo
$$-$$$: all major credit cards accepted
lunch. dinner. full bar. reservations recommended

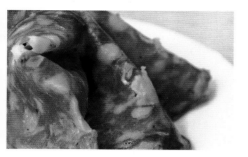

Ladies and gentlemen look no further for that really special, sophisticated yet notably hip restaurant to melt the hardest foodie heart. In fact, a number of my food-obsessed friends, when talking about *Bocca di Lupo,* have a look on their faces that can only be described as glazed rapture. It's a light and airy spot, perfect for the huge Haidee Becker canvasses showcased on the walls. Frankly, I would happily sit in the dankest cave to eat these dishes, each of which announces its regional provenance both on the menu and the palate.

imbibe / devour:
negroni sbagliato
colterenzio pinot nero classico
shaved radish, celeriac & pecorino salad
crescentini with finocchiona & squacquerone
tripe with guanciale, chili & tomato
pork cheeks braised in milk, orange & bay
brioche 'sandwich' of pistachio, chestnut & hazelnut gelati

brindisa shop

spanish food importers' shop in borough market

the floral hall, stoney street se1 9af. opposite park street. tube: london bridge
020.7407.1036 www.brindisa.com
tue - thu 10a - 5.30p fri 10a - 6p sat 8.30a - 5p

opened in 2000. owner: monika linton
$-$$: visa. mc
grocery. deli. first come, first served

borough >

It's a pilgrimage for those who love food, going to *Brindisa*—even without the other myriad delights of Borough Market to tickle your taste buds. As with any pilgrimage, it pays to be prepared. I always have an exhaustive list and plan of attack, which includes upon arrival, having a hot chorizo and rocket roll from the barbecue straight away. This is essential to stop me peckishly impulse-buying the entire shop, having of course left the list on my bedside table. You should know that *Brindisa* has a rather fine tapas bar nearby too, which completes the experience.

imbibe / devour:
joselito gran reserva jamon
dehesa de extremadura jamon
leon cooking chorizo
fresh padron peppers
judion butter beans
torta de aciete fennel seed biscuits
best range of spanish cheese in london
hot chorizo & rocket rolls

caravan

restaurant, bar and coffee roastery

11 - 13 exmouth market ec1r 4qd. corner of pine
tube: farringdon or angel
020.7833.8115 www.caravanonexmouth.co.uk
mon - fri 8a - midnight sat 10a - midnight sun 10a - 4p

opened in 2010. owner / chef: miles kirby
owners: chris ammerman, laura harper-hinton and jedediah coleman
$$: all major credit cards accepted
breakfast. lunch. dinner.   brunch. coffee / tea. full bar. reservations accepted

farringdon > **e07**

Occasionally you make a friend on sight, before they've uttered a word, don't you find? You just get on with it, without the usual preamble. Well, *Caravan* has become one of those instant friends, one I can drop in on any time of the day or evening for anything from breakfast to a nightcap. There's something about it that reminds me of *Elk In The Woods*, which is a good friend featured in the first edition. Exmouth Market already had way more than its fair share of excellent food with *Moro*, *Metcalf* and *The Ambassador*, and now there's *Caravan*: the feisty new kid on the block.

imbibe / devour:
affogato
aceh tenga filter coffee from sumatra
two crumpets & too much butter
caravan fry up
spicy pork-filled, honey-glazed gypsy bun
pickled mackerel, corn, avocado & pea shoots
steamed mussels in green thai coconut curry
wiltshire rainbow trout, sweet potato & chermoula

cocomaya

fine chocolatier and artisan baker

bakery: 12 connaught street w2 2af. corner of porchester place
chocolate shop: 3 porchester place w2 2af. corner of connaught street
tube: marble arch
020.7706.2770 www.cocomaya.co.uk see website for hours

opened in 2008. owners: joel bernstein, walid al damirji and serena rees
$$: all major credit cards accepted
lunch. brunch. treats. coffee / tea. first come, first served

marylebone > e08

I can't believe that it took *eat.shop* research to lead me to *Cocomaya*. How could I never have tasted their amazing pistachio and chocolate croissants? Did I not notice the cheese-straw-shaped hole in my universe? Now that I have discovered the twin delights of *Cocomaya's* artisan bakery and the adjacent chocolate 'lounge,' I shall be joining the fragrant ladies of this well-heeled part of town on a regular basis for lunch. Or even better, a treat or two (or three), of their baked goods and chocolates par excellence.

imbibe / devour:
hot chocolate
cardamon chocolates
jasmine chocolates
russian tea cake
chocolate custard morning cake
cherry brioche with almond cream
rugalach
seasonal salads for lunch

comptoir libanais

lebanese canteen and deli

65 wigmore street w1u 1pz. between st christopher's and marylebone lane
tube: bond street
020.7935.1110 www.lecomptoir.co.uk
mon - fri 8a - 10p sat - sun 10a - 10p

opened in 2009. owner: tony kitous
$: visa. mc
breakfast. lunch. dinner. treats. grocery. coffee / tea. first come, first served

marylebone > e09

I suspect that in years to come *Comptoir Libanais* may become a bigger part of the cityscape with outlets here and there, but for now it is such an original, so beautifully and comprehensively charming, that I find myself, in the manner of my dog Harry, rolling over and wagging my tail in joyful submission. Metaphorically speaking, so far at least. The fresh, bud-tickling Lebanese food, the bright, breezy decor and the joy of an easy-going bite in this part of town have won me over. It must be said that I find myself in this part of town quite a bit more now that *Comptoir Libannais* has arrived.

imbibe / devour:
roomana lemonade with pomegranate & orange blossom
lebanese salad
falafel & fattoush salad with sumak dressing
lamb samboussek
baba ghanuj
tabbouleh salad
shabyat cream

dong san

swish korean restaurant

47 poland street w1f 7nb. between d'arblay and noel streets. tube: oxford circus
020.7287.0997 www.dongsan88.com
mon - sun noon - midnight

opened in 2009. owner: mr. kim. chef: a different mr. kim
$-$$: all major credit cards accepted
lunch. dinner. wine / beer. reservations accepted

**soho > **

Since I love kimchi and Korean restaurants are suddenly everywhere in London, I made it my mission to find a great one. After much kimchi consumpion, I found the place: *Dong San.* Picture the scene. It's lunchtime and I am simultaneously eating and taking pictures of lovely, spicy Korean dishes, when I hear screaming and whoops of joy. South Korea has just scored against mighty Brazil in the World Cup. Being a sucker for drama, I create my own and imagine that South Korea ends up winning the Cup and I become an honorary Korean. I think kimchi must have hallucinogenic powers.

imbibe / devour:
cinnamon punch
jasmine tea
bibimbap
kimchi chige
savoury dried cabbage with beef ribs stew
tempura
bulgogi
beef & octopus chungol

fernandez & wells

a deli, a cafe and a wine bar in soho

43 lexington street w1f 9al. between beak and broadwick streets

tube: oxford circus

020.7734.1546 www.fernandezandwells.com

see website for hours and additonal locations

opened in 2007. owners: jorge fernandez and rick wells

$-$$: visa. mc

breakfast. lunch. brunch. coffee / tea. wine. deli. first come, first served

soho >

The duo behind *Fernandez & Wells* know what makes Soho tick—great coffee, glorious food and, after work, a bottle of good wine with delicious things to nibble. The Lexington location is a deli by day, wine bar by night while 'round the corner on Beak Street is the coffee shop. Now, hurrah, they have added a third string to their bow in nearby St. Anne's Court with a daytime coffee shop and, of course, delicious food to match. When the sun goes down this place slips into something more comfortable, with wine and charcuterie. The *Fernandez & Wells* seduction is complete.

imbibe / devour:
coffee roasted by
  stephen leighton of hasbean
08 jean defaix chablis
roast chicken ciabatta
slow roast pulled pork sandwich
pasteis de nata
chelsea bun
platter of cheeses

fields

a fine deli for a picnic
15 corsica street n5 1jt. at calabria road. tube: highbury & islington
020 7704 1247
mon - fri 9a - 8p sat 9.30a - 6.30p sun 10a - 5p

opened in 2004. owner: shiraz maneksha
$-$$: all major credit cards accepted
grocery. coffee / tea. wine / beer. first come, first served

islington > 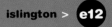 e12

I liked the owner of *Fields* even before I met her because of the care and detailed thought that had obviously gone into the foods on display here. It's clear Shiraz is a real foodie, with not only good taste, but a sense of social responsibility. Were I based in this 'hood, there's no doubt I would live out of this shop, but since I'm not, it will be my spot for putting together a great picnic for a sunny day on Highbury Fields. Since they offer a hamper service, I might even pre-order mine, removing every last bit of stress from my relaxing dream day.

imbibe / *devour:*
taylors of harrogate teas & coffees
artisan wines from italy
locally baked bread
homemade cakes
all-organic fruit, vegetables & herbs
eggs, milk & butter straight from the (welsh) farm
pre-ordered meat delivered straight from the
    farm to the shop

fino

beloved spanish restaurant

33 charlotte street (entrance on rathbone street) w1t 1rr. at charlotte place
tube: goodge street or tottenham court road
020.7813.8010 www.finorestaurant.com
mon - fri noon - 2.30p, 6 - 10.30p sat 6 - 10.30p

opened in 2003. owners: sam and eddie hart. chef: nieves barragon
$$-$$$: all major credit cards accepted
lunch. dinner. full bar. reservations recommended

fitzrovia >  **e13**

Welcome aboard the good ship *Fino,* and what a beloved ship she is. This is a cruise I would book, no question. There is something so wonderfully assured about the whole *Fino* experience—the food from Nieves' kitchen, the wine list, the staff, the surroundings—you feel that the great gods of restaurants have smiled on this place and therefore on you. Of course, what that actually means is that Sam and Eddie Hart are consummate restauranteurs, their talents on display not only here, but also their Soho tapas bar *Barrafina* and now at *Quo Vadis* too.

imbibe / devour:
pisco sour cocktail
fabulous wine & sherry list
crisp pork belly
razor clams
chick peas, spinach & roast pancetta
picos, celery & walnut salad
chipirones
stuffed courgette flowers

fleet river bakery

a cool café

71 lincoln's inn fields wc2a 3jf. corner of gate street and twyford place
tube: holborn
020.7691.1457 www.fleetriverbakery.com
mon - fri 7a - 6p sat 9a - 4p

opened in 2009. owners: lucy clapp and jon dalton. chef: julie grant
$: visa. mc
breakfast. lunch. brunch. treats. coffee / tea. wine / beer. first come, first served

holborn > **e14**

Fleet River Bakery is tucked away and very easy to miss, which might explain why I had never seen it though it's mere yards from my regular cycle cut-through. When the fourth person insisted I go here I said "enough, already" and sought it out. I thank them all for pointing me to this little gem which is now a regular drop in—though I avoid the wage-slave lunch hour queue. All in all, *Fleet River* is heaven, and the scrumptious tea time cake-fest I had here the other day was all the sweeter for knowing I would work a good, ooh, tenth of it off on the cycle home.

imbibe / devour:
monmouth coffee
homemade chai latte
scrambled eggs on sourdough toast with bacon
scones with cream & strawberry jam
feta & sun-dried tomato frittata
hummingbird cake
banana & walnut cake
chocolate cake

franco manca

artisan pizza in a covered market
unit 4, market row sw9 8ld. between electric avenue and coldharbour lane
tube: brixton (see website for address of second location in chiswick)
020.7738.3021 www.francomanca.co.uk
mon - wed, fri - sat noon - 5p thu noon - 10p

opened in 2008. owners: giuseppe mascoli and sami wasif. chef: alfonso marseglia
$: all major credit cards accepted
lunch. dinner (thu). wine / beer. first come, first served

brixton >

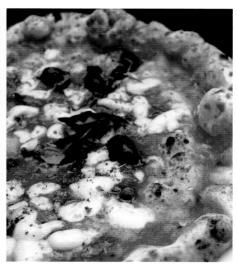

There's been a pizzeria in Brixton's covered market for many years. When I lived nearby it was *Franco's*, which was good. Now it's become *Franco Manca* and it's fabulous. The sublime pizzas are miraculously both crispy and chewy at the same time, made from slow-rising sourdough baked in wood-burning ovens and topped with organic vegetables and rare breed meats. I'm happy to tell you that the market still throbs with energy and the people-watching here is still second to none. Some things never change.

imbibe / devour:
organic dolcetto wine
sam smith organic beer
seasonally changing pizzas:
 tomato, capers, anchovy & mozzarella.
 tomato, cured organic chorizo & mozzarella
 home-cured gloucester old spot ham,
  mozzarella & tomato
mozzarella, buffalo ricotta & wild mushrooms

gelateria danieli

handmade italian ice cream

16 brewers lane tw9 1hh. between george street and the green
tube, overground or rail: richmond
020.8439.9807 www.gelateriadanieli.com
see website for other locations and seasonal hours

opened in 2005. owner: carlo vagliasindi. chef: bridget hunt
$: cash only
treats. first come, first served

richmond >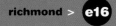

Great ice creams I have eaten stand out in my memory, usually with a place and particular flavour attached. *Trastavere* in Rome (dark chocolate), *Marine Ices* in Camden (coconut), *Berthillon* in Paris (cassis sorbet) and now *Gelateria Danieli* (pistacchio) located in a cute alleyway in Richmond. As I was taking these pictures with my son Jonjo (that's him licking his lips above), I met the lovely Bridget who devised the recipes, so I now know the passion that goes into this ice cream. After we tried many different flavours, Jonjo and I may feel just as passionately about *Gelateria Danieli.*

imbibe / devour:
flavours include:
  dark chocolate
  stracciatella
  pistacchio
  coconut
  lemon sorbetto
mini cones for litle ones
canestrini (chocolate tub cones)

ginger & white

coffee and food with style

4a - 5a perrins court nw3 1qs. between heath street and hampstead high street
tube: hampstead
020.7431.9098 www.gingerandwhite.com
mon - fri 7.30a - 5.30p sat - sun 8.30a - 5.30p

opened in 2009. owners: emma scott, nicholas scott and tonia george
chef: jessica mayer-jones
$-$$: visa. mc
breakfast. lunch. brunch. treats. coffee / tea. first come, first served

hampstead >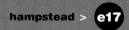

I have always had a soft spot for Hampstead, with its excellently eccentric seniors (a very high-quality boho intellectual band of elderly conversationalists) and its long-standing café culture. Now Hampstead has gone all foodie to boot, what with the lovely *Melrose & Morgan* deli opening a branch, and *Gail's* on the High Street, as well as the rather wonderful *Ginger & White*, tucked into a charming alleyway. This is a perfect café to have a good cup of coffee and something delicious to eat while you chat, write or simply muse the afternoon away, in true Hampstead style.

imbibe / devour:
square mile coffee roasters' coffee
montezuma's hot chocolate infused with chili
soft boiled eggs & dippy soldiers
porridge with winter berries & cinnamon
wicks manor smoked ham & quickes cheddar
   on potato & rosemary bloomer
lemon drizzle cake
victoria sponge cake

j & a café

hidden cafe restaurant

4 sutton lane ec1m 5pu. between great sutton street and clerkenwell road
(entrance opposite the slaughtered lamb). tube: farringdon or barbican
020.7490.2992 www.jandacafe.co.uk
see website for hours

opened in 2008. owners: johanna, aoife and jp ledwidge
$-$$: visa. mc
breakfast. lunch. brunch. treats. coffee / tea. full bar. first come, first served

clerkenwell > **e18**

Things started well as Affy at *SCP* (see shop section) looked through the first edition of this book murmuring his approval of my choice of cafés. He then began suggesting places, each of which I already loved and had shot for this edition. He's obviously got great taste. Then he said, eyes ablaze, "Aha! What about that fantastic hidden place, *J & A Cafe*?" And I knew we'd struck gold. This place is a gem, from the classic *J & A* breakfast, through lunches and teatime cakes, to evenings drinking wine in the oyster bar upstairs. Many thanks, Affy.

imbibe / devour:
j. atkinson & co. teas & coffees
a glass of sauvignon blanc
j & a breakfast
smoked salmon & scrambled eggs on
  freshly baked irish soda bread
pan fried lemon & crushed pepper
  chicken breast salad with avocado
half a dozen maldon oysters

konstam

seriously seasonal restaurant within an old pub building

2 acton street (at the prince albert) wc1x 9na. corner of king's cross
tube: king's cross
020.7833.5040 www.konstam.co.uk
see website for hours

opened in 2006. owner / chef: oliver rowe
$$-$$$: all major credit cards accepted
lunch. dinner. brunch. full bar. reservations recommended

king's cross > e19

I have long heard of the virtues of hogget so I gave a whoop of gastro joy to find it on *Konstam's* menu. Hogget (come on, you want to know now, admit it) is sheep's meat between one and two years old, so it's between lamb and mutton and it's super delicious. Mind you, Oliver Rowe is, I believe, the culinary equivalent of a supermodel who'd look great in a bin bag and is able to make anything taste sensational. This is handy for any chef who prides himself on his fully seasonal menus and sourcing 80% of ingredients from within the Greater London area.

imbibe / devour:
local beers
chilled beetroot soup with chopped egg
braised shank of amersham hogget with
   herb barley, herring & nasturtium relish
pan fried mersea seabass with fried potatoes
asparagus, chard and spätzle gratin
waterloo cheese, roast onion chutney & toast
lemon and lavender posset

lantana

good coffee and fresh food melbourne style

13 charlotte place w1t 1sn. between charlotte and goodge streets
tube: goodge street or tottenham court road
020.7637.3347 www.lantanacafe.co.uk
see website for hours

opened in 2008. owners: shelagh and caitlin ryan, michael homan and alex wingate
chef: reagan ellenbroek
$-$$: visa. mc
breakfast. lunch. brunch. coffee / tea. wine / beer. first come, first served

fitzrovia >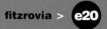

My love affair with the Antipodean lifestyle, or should I say foodstyle, continues, albeit at as large a distance as is possible without launching into space travel. I just love the Aussie touch, with that obsessive attention to the detail of every bean and berry. Here at *Lantana*, the vibe is pure Melbourne, I'm told, though for me it's a purely chilled out, London thing. I love the fact that *Lantana* has put its takeaway counter in the building next door, so that even at lunchtime the relaxed ambiance doesn't get stressed by the worker ant queue.

imbibe / devour:
bloody mary
chinotto
poached eggs with a sicilian ratatouille
toasted muesli with grated apple & yoghurt
corn fritters stacked with bacon, rocket,
  corn salsa & lime aioli
sesame crusted pork loin with asian greens
  and sweet & sour onion relish

look mum no hands!

café, bar and bike workshop
49 old street ec1v 9hx. opposite domingo street
tube: barbican
020.7253.1025 www.lookmumnohands.com
mon - fri 7.30a - 10p sat 9a - 10p

opened in 2010. owners: att harper, sam humpheson and lewin chalkley
$-$$: visa. mc
breakfast. lunch. dinner. coffee / tea. wine / beer. first come, first served

clerkenwell > **e21**

I spotted *Look Mum No Hands!* right before it opened for business, and even at the end of a hard eating and shopping day I could see that this great site had potential to become a nice place for a pie and a beer. And there's the added charm of watching Nic mend bikes with expert ease, as all manner of racers and tandems rock up to feel her love. Some people even walk here, would you believe it? The bike repair / café marriage seems to be a happy one, with *Towpath, Lock 7* and now with *Look Mum No Hands!* forming a trinity of hip puncture hospital hangouts.

imbibe / devour:
square mile coffee
earl grey blue flower tea
aspalls organic cyder
slag & vedett beers
beef steak & stilton pie
spinach, feta & pine nuts pie
spinach, goat cheese & sun-dried tomato panier
crumpet with marmite

mrs marengo's

flesh-free delights

53 lexington street w1f 9as. between beak and broadwick streets
tube: oxford circus
020.7287.2544 www.mrsmarengos.co.uk
mon - fri 8a - 6p sat noon - 6p

opened in 2008. owner: jane muir. chef: robert watson
$-$$: visa. mc
breakfast. lunch. brunch. treats. grocery. coffee / tea. first come, first served

soho > e22

I am, to be honest, amazed. My friend Al 'The Fire,' a chef manqué if ever there was one, tells me that I have to go to *Mrs Marengo's*. He raves about the full English breakfast, the burgers, the salads. So, of course, I go and I love it. The breakfast is phenomenal, the lunch salads the stuff of legend and the cupcakes positively wink with flirtatious cheek. But the amazing thing is that Al, a dyed-in-the-wool carnivore, never once mentioned to me that *Mrs Marengo's* is completely and utterly vegetarian. I'm not sure that there is a finer accolade.

imbibe / devour:
berrimango smoothie
poached eggs with tomatoes, beans,
  mushrooms, veggie sausages & toast
granola with almonds, pecan & cranberries
red kidney bean burger, jalapeño, coriander &
  carrot with sweet potato fries
wild mushroom, goats cheese & ricotta cake
photocakes to order

needoo grill

sensational punjabi restaurant

87 new road e1 1hh. between fieldgate and fordham streets. tube: whitechapel

020.7247.0648 www.needoogrill.co.uk

mon - sun 11a - 11p

opened in 2009. owner / chef: mushtaq ali

$: visa. mc

lunch. dinner. byob. reservations accepted

whitechapel >  **e23**

It is a source of great hilarity to Simon, my partner, that I used to dance in my seat when eating really good food. Unconsciously, I hasten to add. Well, these days I tend to express my delight more verbally, unless I'm at *Needoo Grill*, where the spicy tongue dish creates flavorful explosions in my mouth and the incredible peshwari nan has me getting my buttocks in boogie mode. Mushtaq, the owner, was a longtime manager at the fantastic *Tayyabs* and, like there, you may have to queue to get in, but be patient as you are about to feast, and have a grin from ear to ear.

imbibe / devour:
mango lassi
zeera (salted) lassi
spicy lamb chops
daal baingun
punjabi tinda
chana chicken
needoo peshwari naan
lahori tandoori paratha

nordic bakery

scrumptious scandeliciousness

14a golden square w1f 9jg. between lower john and lower james
tube: piccadilly circus
020.3230.1077 www.nordicbakery.com
mon - fri 8a - 8p sat 9a - 7p sun 11a - 6p

opened in 2007. owner: jali walhsten
$-$$: visa. mc
breakfast. lunch. brunch. treats. grocery. coffee / tea. first come, first served

soho > **e24**

I can't decide if the cinnamon buns from the *Nordic Bakery* constitute a new discovery or a new vice. Let's just say that in the last couple of months I've gone out of my way, and I mean by anything from a minute or two to several miles, to get that special caramelised cinnamon fix. I am forced to admit that these detours happen too often to be merely accidental. I'm dealing with it, ok? Perhaps next time I will have something else with my coffee when I come (way out of my way) to the *Nordic Bakery*. Oh, come on—who am I kidding?

imbibe / devour:
wild blueberry juice
dibar coffee
salmakki salty liquorice
cinnamon buns
gravadlax with dill sauce on rye bread
cheese & pickle on rye
egg & herring on rye
tigercake

nude espresso

dreamy kiwi coffee house

26 hanbury street e2 6qr. between commercial and brick lane
tube: liverpool street / aldgate east or overground: shoreditch high street
www.nudeespresso.com
mon - fri 7.30a - 6p sat - sun 10a - 6p

opened in 2008. owner: richard reed. chef: ceri tinkler
$: visa. mc
breakfast. lunch. brunch. treats. coffee / tea. first come, first served

shoreditch >

Each of the many times I have recommended *Nude Espresso* to someone and I get to the part about the toasted banana bread with the honeycomb salted butter, my mouth waters to the point where I have to stop speaking for a few seconds (it's happening now). Take this as a very good sign. *Nude Espresso* is a super friendly place where coffee obsessives are in heaven as the roastery is in house and the roasters tweak each batch in a quest for the ultimate brew. Did I already say the food is fabulous and you must must must try the toasted banana bread with... ah, hang on a minute.

imbibe / devour:
single estate producer coffees
"east" espresso blend of arabica coffee
    roasted on site
fentimans ginger beer
banana pancake with maple syrup & yoghurt
thai fishcakes with rocket & lime aioli
carrot, walnut & pineapple cake
eggs florentine

paul rothe & son

classic retro sandwich bar and deli
35 marylebone lane w1u 2nn. between bentinck street and hinde mews
tube: bond street
020.7935.6783
mon - fri 8a - 6p sat 11.30a - 5.30p

opened in 1900. owner: paul rothe
$: cash only
breakfast. lunch. coffee / tea. grocery. first come, first served

marylebone > **e26**

What is it about *Paul Rothe & Son* that makes it so very special? It's not just that you feel that you should be wearing a full skirt, with your carriage waiting outside, or the fact that you can buy jams here that you never knew existed, like Tiptree Mulberry. I think it's the easy, unforced English courtesy—good manners as well as good food. *Rothe's* is super calm and gentle, with all manner of interesting regulars coming in. When you leave, you find yourself actually having a nice day, without ever having been toothily instructed to have one. Old style.

imbibe / devour:
bacon sandwiches
sausage sandwiches
homemade soup
salt beef, mustard & dill in a bap (roll)
salad boxes made to order
seggiano sliced porcini in olive oil
wild asparagus in olive oil
tiptree mulberry jams

paxton & whitfield

cheesemongers and grocers

93 jermyn street sw1y 6je. near duke of york street
tube: piccadilly circus
020.7930.0259 www.paxtonandwhitfield.co.uk
mon - sat 9.30a - 6p

opened in 1797. owner: andrew brownsword
$$: visa. mc
grocery. first come, first served

st james >

Making the redoubtable *Neal's Yard Dairy* and *La Fromagerie* look like young buck arrivistes on the cheese scene is *Paxton & Whitfield*, as assured and easy with itself as I would hope to feel at 210 years old. They have linked up with the equally venerable Parisian cheese shop *Androuet* so they now have a whole raft of great French cheeses to complement their impressive English selection. The Late Night Cheese-Up, always accompanied by The Perfect Biscuit Debate, both long-standing traditions in the kitchens I love, are in for a *P & W* perk-up.

imbibe / devour:
cheese:
   fosseway fleece hard ewes cheese
   tunworth award-winning soft cheese
   stinking bishop
a tower of cheeses for a wedding
comb honey
cheese larders
olivewood cheese boards

petersham nurseries

idyllic café and teahouse inside a beautiful plant nursery

church lane, off petersham road tw10 7ag. between river lane and star and garter hill
tube, overground or rail: richmond > then 65 bus from outside the station
020.8605.3627 www.petershamnurseries.com
café: wed - sun noon - 2:30p teahouse: tue - sat 10a - 4.30p sun 11a - 4.30p

opened in 2003. owners: gael and francesco boglione. chef: skye gyngell
$$$: all major credit cards accepted
lunch. treats. tea / coffee. reservations recommended

richmond > 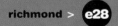 e28

Lunch on a sunny day at *Petersham Nurseries* is the closest thing to a holiday in the South of France you can get without leaving London. Ok, it's technically in Surrey, but then so is Kew Gardens, so don't for a second let that put you off. Walking down pastoral Church Lane you leave the city and enter a world of culinary excellence and astounding wabi sabi beauty. The restaurant, eccentrically called the café, is extremely popular, so the adjoining teahouse is another way to soak up the magic here should you have left it too late to make that all-important reservation.

imbibe / devour:
petersham rose syrup & petals prosecco
homemade amalfi lemonade
risotto with lemon & san daniele
dorset crab with yellow beans & radicchio
grilled quail with heritage tomatoes & lentils
gorgonzola dolce with shaved celery
strawberries & melon with rose geranium posset
chocolate tart with jersey cream

phat phuc noodle bar

vietnamese food in a chelsea courtyard

151 sydney street sw3 6nt. down steps off the corner of king's road
tube: sloane square or south kensington
020.7351.3843 www.phatphucnoodlebar.com
mon - sun noon - 5p

opened in 2001. owners: minky sloane, lexie and ed stoddard
chefs: pon, pai and pom
$: visa. mc
lunch. dinner. wine / beer. first come, first served

chelsea > **e29**

It was said, by a chef of my acquaintance, that the stock base recipe for the pho at *Phat Phuc Noodle Bar* was so closely guarded in the early days that even the owners weren't in on the secret. Nine years later, *Phat Phuc* itself still feels like a bit of a secret. Go down some steps beside a flower vendor and you will find this old-style Saigon street stall nestling in a tranquil courtyard just off the bustling King's Road. Once there, join the regulars for Vietnamese fast food eaten at a leisurely pace. *Phat Phuc*? It means Happy Buddha, of course. What did you think?

imbibe / devour:
jasmine tea
vietnamese coffee
banh cuon
banh xeo
bang bang chicken noodle salad
prawn noodle salad
pho bo
prawn laksa

65

polpo

a soho bacaro

41 beak street w1f 9sb. opposite upper james. tube: oxford circus
020.7734.4479 www.polpo.co.uk
mon - sat noon - 3p, 5.30 - 11p sun noon - 4p

opened in 2009. owners: russell norman and richard beatty. chef: tom oldroyd
$$: all major credit cards accepted
lunch. dinner. full bar. reservations accepted

soho >

I love *Polpo*. There was a time when Beak Street was my playground: my agent's office used to be on this street and my friend Spike ran the nearby *Alphabet bar*. This was before the arrival of *Polpo*, though it's hard to imagine Soho life without it. It pains me to think how many lunchtimes we would have spent devouring the heavenly *bacaro* (back street Venetian bar) food and sipping our way through the wine list. *Polpo* is perfect in every detail, so I give thanks that it is here at last and I intend to sit at the zinc bar to make up for lost time. I suggest you join me.

imbibe / devour:
negroni cocktail
lovely wine list
asparagus, taleggio, prosciutto
salt cod on grilled polenta
broad bean, ricotta & mint bruschetta
calf's liver, onions & sage
risi e bisi
chocolate & orange salami

rock & sole plaice

classic fish and chips

47 endell street wc2h 9aj. corner of shorts gardens. tube: covent garden

020.7836.3785

mon - sun noon - 10.30p

opened in 1871. owners: ali ziyaeddin and ahmet ziyaeddin

$-$$: visa. mc

lunch. dinner. wine / beer. first come, first served

covent garden > e31

As explained in the first edition entry for *The Golden Hind*, fish and chips is not really my idea of a meal out but more of a late-night, stop-gap hangover cure. Or great instant kid food. With this in mind, I intend to bring my kid Jonjo to *Rock & Sole Plaice*, where we will sit outside and feel the balmy breeze waft over us as we eat our crispy battered fish. Yes, it is warm tonight as I write. Were there snow on the ground, we might head to the connoisseur's treat of *Fryer's Delight* on Theobald's Road, where chips are cooked in beef drippings. I'm warm just thinking about it.

imbibe / devour:
cod
haddock
plaice
rock
skate
scampi
onion rings
calamari

ruby

italian inspired food at lunchtime

35 - 42 charlotte road ec2a 3bp. between rivington and great eastern streets
tube: liverpool street / old street or overground: shoreditch high street
mon - fri 7a - 5p sat 10a - 3p

opened in 2006. owner / chefs: leno and afrim
$: cash only
breakfast. lunch. coffee / tea. first come, first served

shoreditch > **e32**

"This is the best food in Shoreditch, bar none," proclaimed a regular proudly as I photographed the lunch he was collecting at *Ruby's*. If I worked in Shoreditch I bet I would come to eat Leno's accomplished Italian cooking every day, too. If you want to eat on premises (worth it, as the banter flows like the coffee) be patient as there are only two tables and one counter on which to perch. I may not yet be a regular but I can already autopilot to *Ruby's* without even realising where my feet are leading me. "Oh, look where I am," I think, "and hungry too! What luck."

imbibe / devour:
1882 caffe vergano coffee
spinach & ricotta tortellini with sage
smoked chicken with couscous
steak sandwich
marinated halloumi &
  roasted hot vegetable sandwich
mushroom & parmesan risotto

saf

sophisticated raw / vegan fine dining
152 - 154 curtain road ec2a 3at. just off corner of old street
tube: liverpool street / old street or overground: shoreditch high street
020.7613.0007 www.safrestaurant.co.uk
see website for hours

opened in 2008. owners: ahan sezer and ersin pamuksuzer
$$-$$$: all major credit cards accepted
lunch. dinner. treats. coffee / tea. full bar. reservations recommended

shoreditch > **e33**

Every time I have eaten at *Saf* I have sat outside, and the sun has always shone, which is odd, this being London. The terrace is lovely with its botanical greenhouse, though inside is just as gorgeous. I would happily sit anywhere at *Saf*, anytime, and bring anyone with me, which in itself is another surprise since half of the menu is raw and the whole menu is utterly, totally vegan. It is also some of the tastiest, most beautiful food you can imagine, as the chefs here have turned vegan cookery into an art form. My taste buds, body and yes, even my soul, give *Saf* thanks at every visit.

imbibe / devour:
madagascar mojito
organic & biodynamic wine list
chilled asparagus soup
sea vegetable salad
pad thai with courgette noodles
lasagne
chocolate ganache
berry cheese cake

sedap

malay / chinese fusion food

102 old street ec1v 9ay. opposite st luke's close
tube: barbican or old street
020.7490.0200 www.sedap.co.uk
mon - fri 11.30a - 2.30p, 6 - 10.30p sat - sun 6 - 10.30p

opened in 2009. owner / chef: mary chong
$-$$: visa. mc
lunch. dinner. byo. reservations accepted

clerkenwell > **e34**

I was sitting at *Sedap*, taking pictures of the delicate, delicious Nyonya (Malay/Chinese fusion) dishes when a group of obviously old friends arrived at the next table and ordered quickly and efficiently. I decided not to eavesdrop and carried on snapping and making notes, while eating, of course. I then changed my mind and let myself actively listen in since they were a) consummate foodies and b) much more entertaining than the water feature next to me. I said hello when I realized that I followed one of them on Twitter. Moral? Londoners who love good food love *Sedap*.

imbibe / devour:
elderflower cordial
teh tarik
malaysian chicken satay
lamb curry with roti prata
kerabu vegetable salad
nasi lemak
sambal brinjal
nyonya kuih

story deli

divinely crispy, 100% organic pizzas

91 brick lane (the old truman brewery) e1 6ql
between quaker street and hanbury street
tube: liverpool street / aldgate east or overground: shoreditch high street
020.7247.3137 www.storydeli.com
mon - sun noon - 10.30p

opened in 2004. owner / chef: lee hollingworth
$$: all major credit cards accepted
lunch. dinner. coffee / tea. wine / beer only. first come, first served

shoreditch > **e35**

Brick Lane will blow your mind with its wealth of shopping, but there will come a point when you need a pit stop, and *Story Deli* is *the* spot. The pizzas are gravity-defying in their lightness and the surroundings are beautiful. Even more so since the recent expansion into this bigger space, which allows the equally wonderful *Story Shop* to join the fold, with all its mysterious treasures to tempt you. Lee and Ann, the *Story* team, have sustainability built their ethos from the bottom up, so you can kick back and enjoy how wonderful a sustainable future can look and taste.

imbibe / devour:
old and new world organic
   wines, beer & cider
pizza:
   parma ham, gorgonzola and spinach
   chorizo & pumpkin pizza
   six cheeses pizza
butterscotch ice cream
elderflower ice cream

terroirs

french wine bar par excellence
5 william iv street wc2n 4dw. between adelaide and agar. tube: charing cross
020.7036.0660 www.terroirswinebar.com
mon - sat noon - 11p

opened in 2008. owner / chef: ed wilson. owners: oli barker and eric nario
$$: visa. mc
lunch. dinner. full bar. reservations recommended

covent garden > **e36**

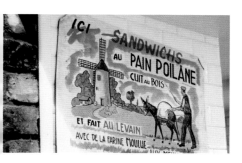

Terroir is one of those impressive, untranslatable French words that packs a punch. It means the specific soil, terrain and microclimatic conditions and their effect on the vine and the wine in the glass. You don't strictly need to know the meaning of this word to have a great meal at *Terroirs* but since you now do, it should alert you to the love and near obsessive care with which they choose their wine list. *Terroirs* champions the smallest artisan viticulteurs producing wines that will melt on your palate. Then they cook the most succulent classic French dishes to go with them. *Zut alors! C'est parfait, merci.*

---

imbibe / devour:
artisan biodynamic & organic wines
petit lucques olives
snails, bacon, garlic & parsley
scottish langoustine & mayonnaise
charcuterie selection
bavette, shallots & red wine
bleu d'auvergne
pannacotta, blood orange & campari

---

the dock kitchen

stevie parle's perfect restaurant

342 / 344 ladbroke grove (portobello dock) w10 5bu. corner of kensal road
tube / overgournd: kensal green or tube: ladbroke grove
020.8962.1610 www.dockkitchen.co.uk
tue - sat noon - 3p, 7.30 - 10.30p

opened in 2009. owner / chef: stevie parle. owner: tom dixon
$$: all major credit cards accepted
lunch. dinner (one sitting only). wine / beer only. reservations recommended

portobello > **e37**

The Dock Kitchen is a total one-off—a design week pop-up in one of Tom Dixon's canalside buildings that has been extended indefinitely. You're buzzed in through a door on an anonymous wall, *Rochelle Canteen* style, immediately making you feel you're in on a wonderful secret. And so indeed you are, though it may not be a secret for long with food this sensational. I had the pilaf, and have cooked variations of it three times in the ten days since, all the while remembering the prodigiously talented Stevie's luscious version. Heaven.

imbibe / *devour:*
homemade hibiscus cordial
08 chianti rufina selvapianna
heritage tomatoes, basil, casteluccio olive oil
   & volpaia vinegar
sicilian aubergine, tomato & seven-spice pilaf
cornish yellow chicken, spiced chickpeas &
   swiss chard
raspberries from chegworth & rose jam fool

the duke of cambridge

organic gastro pub

30 st peter's street n1 8jt. corner of danbury street. tube: angel
020.7359.3066 www.dukeorganic.co.uk
see website for hours

opened in 1998. owner: geetie singh chef: sara berg
$$: visa. mc
lunch. dinner. full bar. reservations accepted

islington >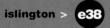

I'm pretty sure I've feted more birthdays at *The Duke of Cambridge* than anywhere else. It's the ideal place to meet up with friends with it's big tables, mismatched chairs and relaxed atmosphere. Anyone who wants to eat can do so, while others can slake their thirst from the draught cider, beer and wine on offer. And *The Duke's* organic credentials are impeccable, which, even before I read "Animal, Vegetable, Miracle" would have meant something. I relish the fact that my Sunday roast here had a natural, pesticide-free existence. *The Duke* makes organic easy and delicious, with no smugness in sight.

imbibe / devour:
chook biodynamic shiraz
luscombe hot ginger beer
st. peter's, pitfield & freedom organic beers
asparagus, broad bean, courgette & pecorino
roast lamb, roasted veg & watercress pesto
pan-fried bream fillet, new potatoes & herb butter
wild boar sausage and mash with onion gravy
custard tart with schnapps fruit

the garrison

pretty, upmarket gastropub

99-101 bermondsey street se1 3xb. corner of white grounds
tube: london bridge
020.7089.9355 www.thegarrison.co.uk
see website for hours

opened in 2003. owners: adam white and clive watson chef: darryl healy
$$: all major credit cards accepted
breakfast. lunch. dinner. tea / cakes. full bar. reservations recommended

bermondsey >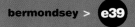

There are great gastropubs in London, lots of them, and then there are fine restaurants within old pub buildings like *Konstam* or *Great Queen Street*. And then there's *The Garrison* which, though it bills itself as a public house, is quite the prettiest pub make-over I've ever seen, and feels, well, nothing like a pub to me. If pubs were all this pleasant, people would hold AA meetings in them. Though the brains behind *The Garrison* are obviously serious about wining and dining their customers, what charms me is that they do it with a twinkle.

imbibe / devour:
breton cider
lots of (mostly old world) wines
salmon three ways with cucumber pickle
spiced glazed pork belly
butternut gnocchi with sauteed mushrooms
raspberry & amaretto trifle
sunday roasts
baked pumpkin & maple cheesecake

the spice shop

the ultimate spice shop

1 blenheim crescent w11 2ee. near corner of portobello road

tube: ladbroke grove

020.7221.4448 www.thespiceshop.co.uk

mon - sat 9.30a - 6p sun noon - 5p

opened in 1995. owner: birgit erath

$: visa. mc

grocery. first come, first served

portobello >

While on my *eat.shop* travels I remembered that my spice trolley (my name is Caroline and I am a spiceaholic) was running low on Yemeni Zhug powder and headed for my old favourite: *The Spice Shop*. I then had a hilariously slow-motion eureka! moment as I reached for the product on the shelf, realising that, of course, you too should know about this wonderful treasure trove for the intrepid taste traveller. It's a cook's dream here and the fact that *Books for Cooks* is opposite makes this, quite possibly, the tastiest road in the capital.

imbibe / devour:
fresh chilies
rose salt
bizar a shuwa from oman
tunisian qualat daqqa
mace blades
burmese chicken curry mix
moroccan raz el hanout
facing heaven chilies

the vintage house

whisky emporium

42 old compton street w1d 4lr. between dean and frith streets
tube: piccadilly circus
020.7437.2592 www.vintagehouse.co.uk
mon - sat 9a - 11p sun 9a - 10p

opened in 1945. owner: malcolm mullin
$-$$$: all major credit cards accepted
first come, first served

soho >

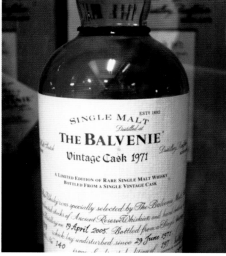

The Vintage House is whisky central, with a vast selection of seriously good rums, tequilas, wines and cigars thrown in for good measure. All of this means so much more to me now that Spike and Hege, both drinks industry experts, have taken my alcoholic education upon themselves. With much patience they unraveled for me the mysteries of stills, aromatics and suchlike, leaving me realizing how much more there is to explore in the wide, wide world of spirits as well as the darker corners and nether regions of *The Vintage House*.

imbibe:
18 year old allt-a-bhainne
18, 20 & 25 year old talisker
'88 château nénin pomerol
ardbeg supernova
diplomatico reserva exclusiva rum
jose cuervo reserva de la famiglia anejo tequila
arette gran clase tequila
cuban cigars

unpackaged

grocery shop with a mission
42 amwell street (the old lloyds dairy) ec1r 1xt. corner of river street
tube: angel or king's cross
020.7713.8368 www.beunpackaged.com
mon - fri 10a - 7p sat 9a - 6p

opened in 2007. owner: catherine conway
$-$$: all major credit cards accepted
grocery. first come, first served

islington >

Catherine is a woman on a mission. She had a very successful stall on the blisteringly hip Broadway Market for a few months, then 'hey, presto!' she found these beautiful premises in Amwell Street and opened this stylish grocery shop with not a carrier bag in sight. Her idea is that you bring your own containers and refill them, though she won't send you away empty handed if you've left yours at home. *Unpackaged* is full of lovely staples, tasty treats and clever eco products, which makes sustainability look so easy that you leave wondering why all shops can't be like this. Foodie fun without the plastic.

imbibe / devour:
chegworth valley juices
samuel smiths lager
born & bread bread
free range eggs
medjool dates
royal ükb jar tops
fresh organic fruit & vegetables
wild mushroom & asparagus pies

viet hoa café

the mother of all east london vietnamese cafés

70 - 72 kingsland road e2 8dp. between cremer and waterson streets
tube: old street or overground: hoxton
020.7729.8293 www.viethoarestaurant.co.uk
mon - fri 7a - 11.30p sat - sun 12.30 - 11.30p

opened in 1996. owners: quyen and hien ly. chef: hoa ly
$-$$: all major credit cards accepted
lunch. dinner. wine / beer only. reservations accepted

shoreditch >

We go back a long way, *Viet Hoa Café* and I. Although this area is now Vietnamtown, years ago this stretch was a food wasteland, with *Viet Hoa* housed inside the Vietnamese Cultural Centre a mile away. Then a fascinating man called Richard fixed up a building, persuaded his friends, *Viet Hoa* included, that they should move in and, boom, a new area was born. Though I may occasionally dally in *Green Papaya* or *Viet Grill*, I always return to the *Viet Hoa* mother ship for the chicken and prawn goi of my dreams.

imbibe / devour:
tsingtao beer
homemade lemonade
summer rolls
banh xeo
bun (spicy soup) with prawns
stir fried chicken with pickled greens
fried tilapia fish with mango

violet cakes

charming baked goods and tea shop

47 wilton way e8 3ed. between lansdown drive and greenwood road
overground: dalston junction or hackney central
020. 7275. 8360 www.violetcakes.com
wed - sat 9:30a - 6p

opened in 2010. owner / baker: claire ptak
$-$$: cash only
coffee / tea. treats. first come, first served

london fields > **e44**

Violet Cakes is impossibly cute. I resisted these cupcakes when they were only available at the Broadway Market stall, but now that *Chez Panisse* alum Claire has opened a storefront I succumb with astonishing ease and regularity. After all what picture is more perfect than a girl sitting, drinking tea and nibbling a cupcake? Oops, I ate that one in two bites—I had better get another. I enjoy watching the baking here also, as the cupcakes come fresh out of the oven, like plump cherubs on parade, about to be issued their iced wings in pastel colours. It makes them even more irresistible, if such a thing were possible.

imbibe / devour:
lots of teas & square mile coffees
scones with clotted cream & baked rhubarb
st john sourdough bread (wed & fri)
courgette & robiola sandwich
asparagus & leek tart with comté
almond polenta cupcakes
chocolate devil's food cupcake with
    marshmallow icing

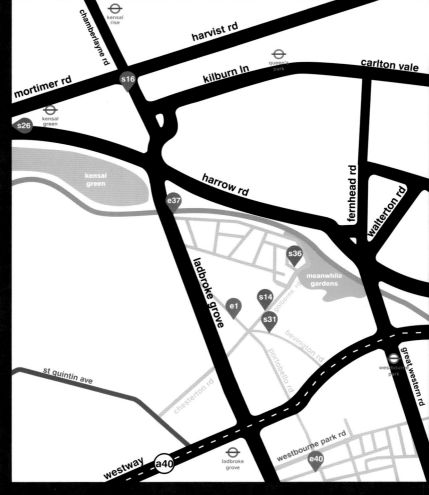

- **portobello**
- **kensal rise**

eat

e1 > anar persian kitchen
e37 > the dock kitchen
e40 > the spice shop

shop

s14 > howie & belle
s16 > kokon to zai
s26 > retrouvius (off map)
s31 > soler
s36 > the convenience store

note: all maps face north

marylebone

eat

e8 > cocomaya
e9 > comptoir libanais
e26 > paul rothe & son

shop

s35 > the button queen
s40 > tracey neuls

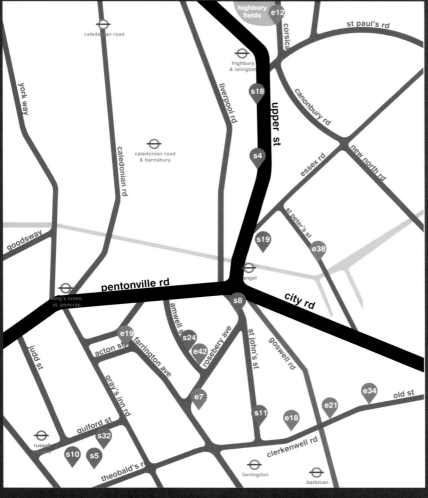

holborn •
islington •
king's cross •
farringdon •
clerkenwell •

eat

e7 > caravan
e12 > fields
e18 > j & a café
e19 > konstam
e21 > look mum no hands!
e34 > sedap
e38 > the duke of cambridge
e42 > unpackaged

shop

s4 > after noah
s5 > ben pentreath
s8 > bobbins bicycles
s10 > darkroom
s11 > ellis+louca
s18 > labour of love
s19 > loop
s24 > pigment & patina
s32 > susannah hunter

note: all maps face north

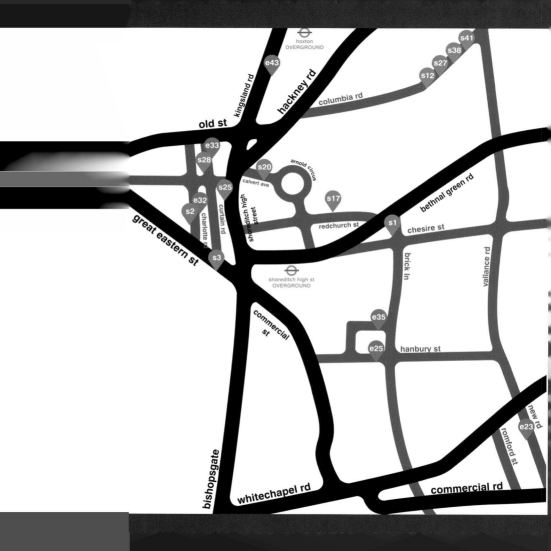

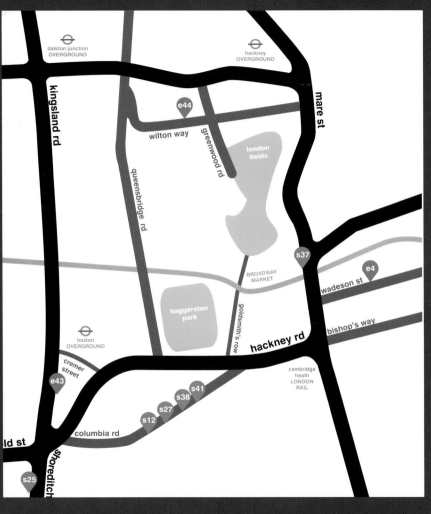

columbia • road
london • fields
bethnal • green

eat

e4 > bistrotheque
e43 > viet hoa café*
e44 > violet cakes

shop

s12 > future vintage*
s25 > present*
s27 > ryantown*
s37 > the last tuesday society
s38 > the powder room*
s41 > wingate studio=shop

* these bizs also appear on the
shoreditch map.

note: all maps face north

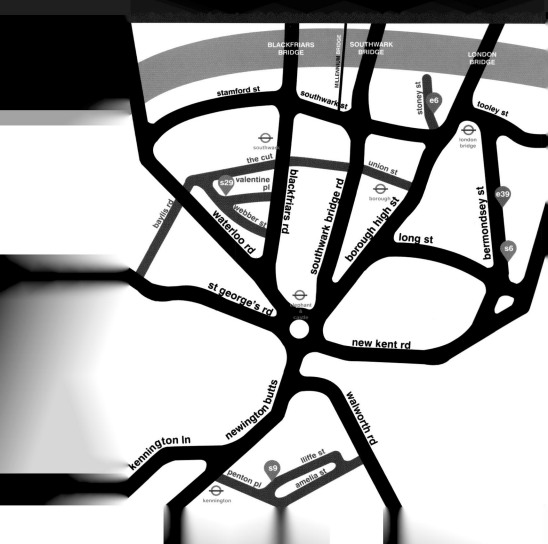

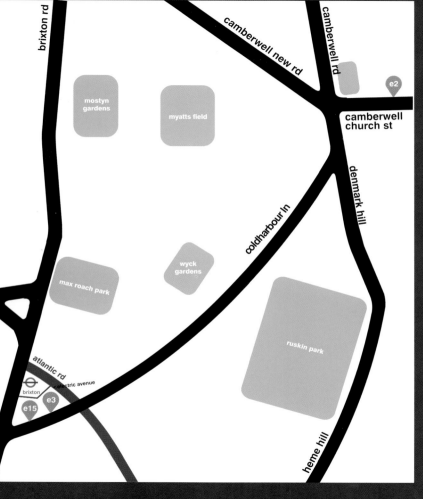

brixton •
camberwell •

eat

e2 > angels & gypsies
e3 > asmara
e15 > franco manca

note: all maps face north

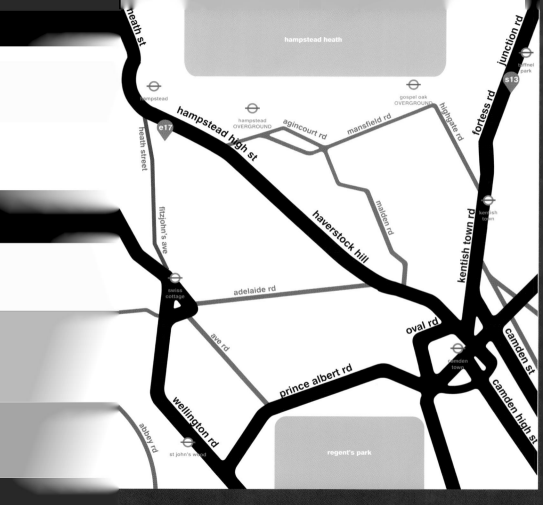

note: all maps face north

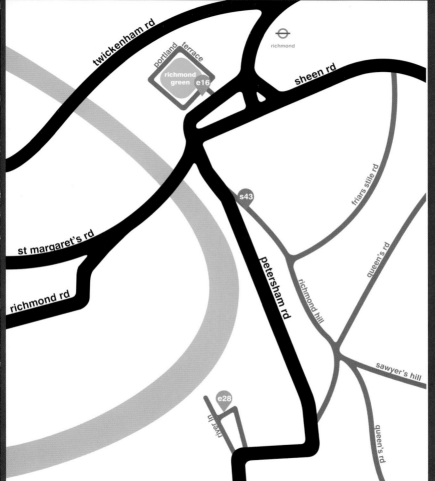

richmond •

eat

e16 > gelateria danieli
e28 > petersham nurseries

shop

s43 > yvonne damant

note: all maps face north

127 brick lane

past and current season avant garde woman's clothing

127 brick lane e1 6sb. between sclater street and bethnal green road
tube: liverpool street / old street or overground: shoreditch high street
020.7729.6320 www.127bricklane.com
mon - sun 11a - 7p

opened in 2005. owners: elisa pensa and fabrizia baldelli
all major credit cards accepted

shoreditch > **s01**

Whenever I pass *127 Brick Lane*, I like to peer in through the window to check out who is in the store. It's become a habit, a sort of game if you like. I can count on one hand the number of browsers not wearing black, for example, though I have long since lost count of how many seriously fashionable Japanese shoppers I have seen flicking through the rails. Placing myself on the other side of the door, I can more fully understood why the chic clientele are drawn to these beautiful pieces of art masquerading as clothes, bags and shoes.

covet:
martin margiela
rick owens
collection privèe
balenciaga
hussein chalayan
charlotte bobeldijk
fannie schiavoni
venom couture

a142

quirky independent women's boutiqe

29 charlotte road ec2a 3pf. between rivington and great eastern streets
tube: liverpool street / old street or overground: shoreditch high street
020.7739.3573 www.a142store.com
mon - fri 11.30a - 6.30p

opened in 2010. owner: debora mccann
visa. mc

shoreditch >

A142 has all the ingredients of my perfect boutique: high ceilings, lots of space to flounce about as you try on eclectic clothing that have buckets of style. This ex-button factory now houses both shop and showroom (to promote the talented designers whose wares are on offer) and Debora, who oozes effortless chic, has made this new space a worthy partner its sister shop in nearby Spitalfields. No surprise, at *A142* I cracked, setting down the camera, breaking my 'no buying on the job' rule after finding a perfect summer dress. You will understand why I weakened when you visit.

covet:
designers remix
pyrus
near far
simeon farrar
bolongaro trevor
the jacksons
humanoid
pallett belben

a child of the jago

provocative menswear shop
10 great eastern street ec2a 3nt. corner of holywell lane
tube: liverpool street / old street or overground: shoreditch high street
020.7377.8694 www.achildofthejago.com
mon - sun 11a - 7p

opened in 2008. owners: joseph corré and simon "barnzley" armitage
all major credit cards accepted

shoreditch >  **s03**

Men, it's your turn. Fashion is meant to be fun, and here at *A Child of the Jago*, it will be, I promise you. This is the spot to release your inner dandy with clothes old and new that all bring something to the party. This brainchild of Joseph (*Agent Provocateur*) Corré, of the Westwood/McLaren style genes, and Simon "Barnzley" Armitage, will be credited in the years to come, when men have boldly stepped out of their boring denim prison back into the freedom of peacockery, with sowing one of the wonderful, rebellious seeds.

covet:
a child of the jago collection:
  l'anarchiste jacket
  3 penny knit jacket
  fighting monkey t's
  hogarth print t's
  stovepipe hat
  orgy shorts & jacket
judy blame jewellery

after noah

a cornucopia of homeware and toys for all
121 upper street n1 1qp. between theberton and almeida streets
tube: angel or highbury & islington
020.7359.4281 www.afternoah.com
mon - sat 10a - 6p sun noon - 5p

opened in 1990
owners: zoe candlin, matthew crawford, nathalie hankey and simon tarr
visa. mc
online shopping. custom orders

islington >

After Noah is, I admit, a little more catholic in its taste than other stripped back *eat.shop* retailers. But that's why I love it so. Here they cater to a multitude of different shopping desires, where anything from a tuppenny chew to a handmade leather sofa can be found, each item lovingly chosen by the quirky, eagle-eyed buyers on staff. So, while you can make the child you've left at home tickled with something from the excellent toy department, be warned that you may emerge with many, many other gifts, including something for yourself, tucked under your arm.

covet:
union jack trunk
robots
nemo sofa range
timber kits mechanical marvels in wood
restored antique furniture
children's games
reconditioned vintage telephones
old fashioned sweeties

ben pentreath ltd

superior things for home and life
17 rugby street wc1n 3qt. just off lamb's conduit. tube: holborn
020.7430.2526 www.benpentreath.com
mon - sat 11a - 6p

opened in 2008. owner: ben pentreath
all major credit cards accepted
online shopping. registries

holborn >  s05

As if there wasn't enough shopping joy around Lamb's Conduit Street, with *Persephone Books*, *Darkroom*, *The English House* and *Folk* among many others. Now there's *Ben Pentreath* to delight the eye and the mind. All manner of well chosen treasures bloom in here, although, if you get an attack of indecision, you could do far worse than the gift vouchers, printed by *Hand & Eye Letterpress*, works of art in themselves. This is precisely why the woman redeeming hers asked if she could keep it, to frame, once she'd spent it on something lovely, of course.

covet:
hand & eye letterpress prints
tessa fantoni boxes
alan powers of judd street wrapping papers
astier de villette candles
hartley green pottery
leeds creamware
les toiles du soleil tea towels
london decoupage pen trays

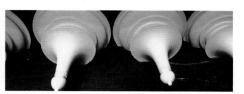

bermondsey 167

clothing and lifestyle shop

167 bermondsey street se1 3uw. between long lane and tanner street
tube: london bridge
020.7407.3137 www.bermondsey167.com
tue - sat 11a - 7p sun noon - 4p

opened in 2007. owner: michael mcgrath
all major credit cards accepted
gallery. bespoke services

bermondsey > s06

One of the discoveries of this latest *eat.shop* journey is that Bermondsey has had a neighborhood make-over in the last few years, with the nearby *Fashion and Textile Museum* to visit and *The Garrison* (see eat section) joining the stalwart Friday antiques market. There is lots to enjoy in Bermondsey these days, but be sure to stroll up the street to take in *Bermondsey 167*, where style comes in all manner of guises, from (ex-Burberry) Michael's own range of beautifully tailored menswear to amazing commissioned, felted flower scarves for women.

covet:
m2cg bespoke & off the peg men's shirts
m2cg lightweight men's knitwear
maria zureta jewellery
pressed paper bench
men's oxidised silver pendants
marco mavilla toywatch
nardis beach women's swimwear
true grace room fragrances

bloomsbury flowers

beautiful balletic blooms

29 great queen street wc2b 5bb. between newton street and drury lane
tube: holborn or covent garden
020.7242.2840 www.bloomsburyflowers.co.uk
mon 9:30a - 5p tue - fri 9.30a - 5.30p sat by appointment only

opened in 1994. owners: stephen wicks and mark welford
all major credit cards accepted
custom orders / design. classes

covent garden > **s07**

Bloomsbury Flowers has long been on my radar and now takes its rightful place in the *eat.shop* pantheon, with its gorgeous blooms, exquisite taste and joyful *je ne sais quoi*. You don't really need to know that Stephen and Mark are ex-Royal Ballet dancers, but this snippet of information does help to explain why this hub of exuberant floral creativity is to be found a mere stone's throw from Covent Garden, incidentally providing the perfect antidote to the austerity of the art deco Freemasons' Hall across the street. What is it about flower shops, I wonder, that makes them such happy places?

covet:
hand-tied bunches
stone containers
potted succulents
roses, of course
orchids
flowers on call
a year in colour collection
bloomsbury boys roadshow

119

bobbin bicycles

beautiful bicycle shop

397 st john street ec1v 4ld. opposite owen street. tube: angel
020.7837.3370 www.bobbinbicycles.co.uk
mon by appointment only tue - fri 11a - 7p sat 11a - 6p sun noon - 5p

opened in 2007. owners: sian emmison and tom morris
visa. mc
online shopping. guided bicycle tours

islington >  s08

TO THE
HELMETS

In *Bobbin's* world ladies can ride bicycles wearing voluminous full skirts since, of course, all *Bobbin* bicycles have chain guards. I've a vision of myself as a *Bobbin* girl, sporting a cape made of Welsh wool, carrying a hip flask and sitting upright, of course. The boys wear brogues and plus fours and we all picnic with lashings of ginger beer. The banal reality of my (t)rusty steed and distinctly unromantic cycling attire is rather less lovely after losing myself in this vision. Yes, I've got serious bicycle envy, I admit it, but *Bobbin Bicycles* will help me through, I know.

covet:
retro styled bicycles:
  pashley
  skeppshult
vintage wool capes
handmade reflective sashes
bicycle bags
wicker baskets
knog frog lights

clements yard

cobbled yard full of creativity
iliffe street, kennington se17 3lj. just off the corner with penton place
tube: kennington
www.clementsyard.com / www.pullensyards.co.uk
first weekend in june and december or by appointment

opened in 1875
cash only
custom orders

kennington >  **s09**

In the 1870s these three yards (Peacock, Iliffe and Clements) were built as Victorian live/work spaces and today they are a living architectural miracle, still hosting a thriving community of all manner of artists and craftspeople. There's loads to experience here, but let's focus for now on *Clements Yard*, with the three talents noted here to whet your appetite. Should you be around for the first weekend in either December or June be sure to check out the *Pullens Yards Open Studios* events which open up all three adjacent yards and offer an unparalleled smorgasbord of creativity.

covet:
ian spencer & cairn young chairs
ian spencer bonifacia too table
adaesi ukairo brass sculptural objects
adaesi ukairo brass wall pieces
carol mather english bull terrier silver brooch
carol mather long-eared jerboa silver salt
    cellar & spoon

darkroom

accesories for men, women and the home

52 lamb's conduit street wc1n 3ll. corner of rugby street. tube: holborn
020.7831.7244 www.darkroomlondon.com
mon - fri 11a - 7p sat 11a - 6p

opened in 2009. owners: lulu roper-caldbeck and rhonda drakeford
visa. mc
online shopping. registries. gift baskets. custom orders. gallery

holborn >

Darkroom is, as they say, a no-brainer for this book and adds another glorious cherry onto the Lamb's Conduit Street cake. This is the place where fashion goes when there are no clothes in sight. What that means, my design-loving friends, is beauty, form and function for you and for your home. Lulu and Rhonda champion designers that they love and admire, shining the light onto their compelling work and letting us take their vision into our lives. This is no doubt a win-win situation all round.

covet:
thomas eyck bags
isaac reina leather satchels
forian jewellery
solomia ceramics
christien meindertsma crocheted poufs
saskia diez jewellery
anglo leather belts
fleet ilya bags

ellis+louca

interiors and design shop

126 st john street ec1v 4js. between clerkenwell road and great sutton street
tube: farringdon
020.7253.4051 www.ellisandlouca.co.uk
mon - fri 10a - 6p sat 10a - 3p

opened in 2010. owner: kally ellis
visa. mc
online shopping. design services

clerkenwell > **s11**

In an ideal world I would move into this shop while Loucas Louca of *Ellis+Louca* redesigns my living space. Don't worry Loucas, take your time, no rush, I'm fine here in the shop, surrounded by all this covetable as well as eminently practical beauty. The farsighted Kally Ellis of *McQueens* flowers fame (round the corner on Old Street) has joined forces with Loucas for this venture and thanks must be given from me, my home and my friends who will undoubtably feel the *Ellis+Louca* benefits for many birthdays and holidays to come.

covet:
shaker inspired side cabinet
kiki gerontaki ceramic tableware
phebus candles
original metal box company
  solar powered nightlights
harrington & squires magnetic shopping list
young kyi wallpaper
lsa handmade vases

future vintage

affordable new and pre-loved designer clothing
98 columbia road e2 7qb. between ravenscroft and gossett streets
tube: liverpool street / old street or overground: shoreditch high street
020.7729.2197 www.future-vintage.co.uk
sat noon - 4p sun 9.30p - 3p

opened in 2008. owner: kate evans
visa. mc

shoreditch >

Just at the end of Columbia Road Flower Market (which happens on Sunday mornings and is well worth a visit) is this rather special little dress agency. Angela Flanders, the perfumier next door, is the mother of Kate, the owner of *Future Vintage*, and one senses that there must be a good taste part of that double helix DNA structure common to both. Kate also owns *Precious*, on Artillery Passage in Spitalfields, which sells new fashion, and at this weekends-only location she intermixes new and nearly-new contemporary designer womenswear at delicious prices. Lucky us.

covet:
pre-loved:
  chloe
  pucci
  marni
  matthew williamson
new:
  dvf
  mcqueen

harrington&squires

letterpress printers and designers
136a fortess road (the corridor) nw5 2hp. between ravely street and brecknock road
tube: tufnell park
020.7267.1500 www.harringtonandsquires.co.uk
by appointment except pre-christmas december weekends

opened in 2005. owners: chrissie charlton and vicky fullick
cash only
online shopping

tufnell park > **s13**

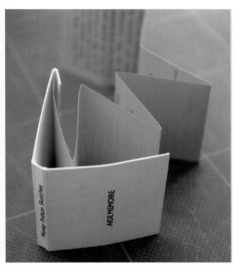

I have just had it confirmed that, yes, my maternal great-grandfather Devitt was 'in the print' during the glory days of Fleet Street. I enjoyed my afternoon at *Harrington&Squires* quirky little premises unravelling the beauty of hand-set type with Chrissie WAY more than was strictly necessary for this gig. I am (no joke) planning to book myself on one of *Harrington&Squires* day courses in the autumn so I too can get inky fingers. Chrissie's love of letterpress is infectious. You have been warned.

covet:
harrington&squires:
  hand printed stationery
  one-off books
  invitations
  calendars
  christmas cards
  commissioned memento boxes
  handkerchiefs

howie & belle

eclectic vintage homeware

52 chamberlayne road nw10 3jh. between mortimer and wakeman roads
tube / overground: kensal green or overground: kensal rise
020.8964.4553 www.howieandbelle.com
mon - sat 10a - 6p

opened in 2007. owners: abbie and jo kornstein
all major credit cards accepted
online shopping. upholstery by arrangement

kensal rise > **s14**

Howie & Belle is one of a Chamberlayne Road triumverate of cool antique shops (the other two being *Circus* and *Niche Antiques*) all within a hundred yards, each with its own very distinct character. At *Howie & Belle*, Abbie and Jo make you feel like you're in the landscape of a narrative, an old tale, with lampshades floating in air over your head and precious things to fall in love with all around you. If they had a spinning wheel in here I would try my very best not to touch it, but I fear that I wouldn't be able to resist.

covet:
vintage sign letters
cake stands
vintage furniture & lampshades
vintage clothes
customized french domes
old organ stops
silk uphostered french beds
vintage mirrors

john lobb ltd

bespoke, handmade-to-measure shoes
9 st james's street sw1a 1ef. between king and pall mall. tube: green park
020.7930.3664 www.johnlobbltd.co.uk
mon - fri 9a - 5.30p sat 9a - 4.30p

opened in 1849. owner: john hunter lobb
all major credit cards accepted
online shopping. custom orders / design

st james > **s15**

Time stops in *John Lobb's*. The wooden 'lasts' of each customer's feet are still carved by hand, as they have always been, the bespoke shoes still perfect in every detail, and the clock's ticking sounds loud in this atmosphere of total concentration. Even the entrance of a random ranting man while I was taking these pictures failed to ruffle the calm, with a quietly spoken "What a strange man" from one of the craftsmen after he had left restoring the focus. This degree of care must surely transfer itself to the pristine leather pieces of art created here, and thus to the feet of the lucky wearer, no?

covet:
any style of shoe, boot or slipper in leather
   made to order
shoe & boot trees made to order
wallets
attaché cases
shoe cleaning boxes
spats
boot hooks

kokon to zai

funky clothing, accessories and objects
86 golborne road w10 5ps. opposite swinbrook road.
tube: ladbroke grove
020.8960.3736 www.kokontozai.co.uk
mon - sat 10a - 6p

opened in 2008. owners: sasha bezovski and marjan pejoski
all major credit cards accepted
online shopping. custom design

portobello >

I love the fact that Sasha at *Kokon To Zai* raved to me as much about the mad cards, made from old photographs adulterated by a 13 year-old girl, as he did about the amazing clothes and jewellery here. His eclectic imagination fills this fascinating ex-butcher's shop with strange wonders, and an entirely different vibe than its Soho sister shop which has for years dispensed its own brand of clubby cool. Golborne Road is a great destination for shopping, Moroccan food and Portuguese style coffee and pastries. Just don't miss the *Kokon To Zai* world while you're here.

covet:
clothes by marjan pejoski, ktz &
 vivienne westwood
marjan pejoski carved hangers
jonni ramli jewellery
yura russian jewellery
mongolian crochetted cotton bedspreads
tribal pieces from afghanistan & borneo
undergrowth ceramic tableware

labour and wait

timeless homeware

85 redchurch street e2 7dj. between brick lane and chilton street
tube: liverpool street / old street or overground: shoreditch high street
020 7729 6253 www.labourandwait.co.uk
tue - sun 11a - 6p

opened in 2000. owners: simon watkins and rachel wythe-moran
visa. mc
online shopping

shoreditch > s17

Labour and Wait, is the first shop I thought of when Kaie, the *eat.shop* publisher, invited me to write the first edition of this book. It is, for me, the most quintessentially *eat.shop* shop in London, as well as unquestionably my favourite retail experience. Its curated perfection is a thing of such beauty I can only urge you to visit it's new Redchurch Street location and let *Labour and Wait*, quite literally, change your life for the better. God is in the detail, they say. With *Labour and Wait* at her elbow, I add.

covet:
wood handled secateurs
black olive oil soap
vintage kitchenware
lemon zester
bakelite pencil sharpeners
welcome doormat
enamel coffee pots
sussex trug

139

labour of love

gorgeous retro-influenced boutique

193 upper street n1 1rq. south of islington park street. tube: highbury & islington
020.7354.9333 www.labour-of-love.co.uk
mon - fri 11a - 6.30p sat 10.30a - 6.30p sun noon - 5.30p

opened in 2005. owner: francesca forcolini
all major credit cards accepted
online shopping

islington > **s18**

I love the fact that you have to look for a bygone shop called *Berwick* in order to find this boutique so beloved by London fashionistas. It's emblematic of the way *Labour of Love* should never be taken at face value. I know that I'm not the only person that has mistakenly assumed that this shop sold only vintage clothing. Then I visited and realized there's a wonderful fusion of today and yesterday on display here. What you might think is something from yesteryear, may well be a modern interpretation. In looking back, there's alot of fashion-forward magic happening here.

covet:
labour of love label
manous
kind
peter jensen
miriam ocariz
tba
eugenia kim
georgina baker jewellery

loop

wool, yarn and textile house of treasures
15 camden passage n1 8ea. between charlton place and islington high street
(opposite pierrepont arcade) tube: angel
020.7288.1160 www.loopknitting.com / www.loopknitlounge.com
tue - sat 11a - 6p sun noon - 5p

opened in 2005. owner: susan cropper
visa. mc
online shopping. classes

islington > **s19**

Loop is lovely. I speak as a knitter, of sorts. I can knock out a kid's scarf, on big needles with fat wool, once a year. It's a start. If ever I had an inspiration to go further, it's *Loop*, with their classes, their blog and incredible selection of exquisite hand-dyed yarns in wools, silks and cottons. There has been a recent explosion of gorgeous craft shops in London—*Beyond Fabrics*, *Our Patterned Hand* and *The Papered Parlour* have all caught my eye, but the one that has reeled me in is the luscious *Loop*.

covet:
yarns:
  malabrigo from uruguay
  madelinetosh
  handmaiden
  koigu hand-dyed
julie arkell papier maché & knit sculptures
sophie digard handknitted scarves
haberdashery & buttons

luna & curious

eclectic design collective
24-26 calvert avenue e2 7jp. corner of bacon street
tube: liverpool street / old street or overground: shoreditch high street
www.lunaandcurious.com
mon - sun noon - 6p

opened in 2006. owners: rhianna lingham, polly george and kaoru parry
all major credit cards accepted
online shopping. custom orders / design. gallery

shoreditch >  **s20**

Luna & Curious is a power surge of creativity and flair in the guise of a shop. This collective of talented designers and artists comes up with all manner of witty wonders and then they present them to us with aplomb. What could be better? Only bigger premises for them to fill with their special magic. By the time you read this in print, *L & C* will be in their new Shoreditch home and I will be able to get a jolt of inspiration from *Luna & Curious* on a regular basis, with the potential for a caffeine jolt from *Leila's* across the road as well.

covet:
lucy jenkins roadkill bracelet
polly george ceramics
we love kaoru ceramics
rhianna lingham jewellery
jane howarth seagull art taxidermy
les queues de sardines hosiery
karin andreasson headpieces
fantastical eyelashes

mint vintage

fresh vintage clothing

20 earlham street wc2 h9ln. between tower street and st martin's lane
tube: covent garden or leicester square
020.7836.3440 www.mintvintage.co.uk
mon - wed 11a - 7p thu - sat 11a - 8p sun noon - 6p

opened in 2005. owner: james wright
all major credit cards accepted
online shopping. occasional alterations

covent garden > **s21**

There is much great vintage around in London at the moment but it often involves a rummage, the thrill of the chase and sometimes a torch. Not so at *Mint Vintage*, where all the digging and de-mustifying has been taken care of, leaving you to try out different looks and accessory combinations. There's a pleasing 50/50 split between menswear and womenswear, so you and s/he can do simultaneous shopping.The helpful staff really know their stock too, making finding exactly what you want a doddle at *Mint*.

covet:
vintage:
  floral men's shirts
  men's french canadian workwear
  '80s inspired dresses
  vintage & collectable sunglasses
  belts
  braces
  shoes, shoes, shoes

mungo & maud

chic, understated accessories for dogs and cats

79 elizabeth street sw1w 9pj. corner of chester row
tube: victoria or sloane square
020.7022.1208 www.mungoandmaud.com
mon - sat 10a - 6p

opened in 2005. owner: nicola sacher
all major credit cards accepted
online shopping

victoria >

I should have taken Harry the dog with me when I visited *Mungo & Maud*. He would have blended in beautifully in this elegantly muted landscape with his blue brindle coloring. And it would have been entertaining to take a bit of lurcher, mixed-race spirit into Belgravia, land of the pedigree mutt. While I was taking pictures a lady came in looking for a bigger collar for her rapidly growing Spaniel puppy, who caused instant joyful havoc, wrestling the toys and jumping onto the beds. Puppies will be puppies, no matter how blue the blood.

covet:

mungo & maud:
    organic cotton & leather labrador collars
    plaited leather collars
    cashmere pullovers (not for you, for fido)
    teflon coated quilted dog coats
    petite amande dog shampoo
    'i'm just walking the dog' wool blanket
    ceramic dog bowl

phonica

superior record shop for vinyl tunes

51 poland street w1f 7lz. opposite d'arblay street. tube: oxford circus
020.7025.6070 www.phonicarecords.com
mon - wed, sat 11a - 7.30p thu - fri 11:30a - 8p sun noon - 6p

opened in 2003. owner: the vinyl factory
visa. mc
online shopping

soho > s23

Remember when record shops reveled in intimidating the uninitiated? Remember that goth's look of pain when you asked for "Happy Talk?" Well, times have changed. *Phonica* is the friendliest place to delve into dance music you could possibly imagine. You can hum whatever tune you want with impunity in here, I promise. London excels in indy record shops with the peerless *Rough Trade*, *Harold Moore* for classical and *Ray's Jazz* as well as the vinyl-tastic *Phonica* where they serve up beats in all manner of guises from afro to wonky, always with charm.

covet:
musical styles sold on vinyl:
  broken beats
  afrobeat
  nu jazz
  techno
sennheiser cans
technics decks
chill pill portable speakerss

pigment & patina

antique painted french furniture, objets and paint effects

48 amwell street ec1r 1xs. between river and inglebert streets
tube: angel or king's cross
020.7833.0650 www.pigmentandpatina.com
tue - sat 10a - 6p

opened in 2010. owners: stephan oberwegner and nicolas carr-forster
visa. mc
online shopping. registries. custom orders / design

islington > s24

Pigment & Patina makes me want to buy a house in France. I'm half French, so maybe the gorgeous things here have a particular pull for me, but I think the seductive beauty of this place would melt the hardest heart. This is shabby chic, French style—way more chic than shabby. The beauty of the things in *Pigment & Patina* comes from the quality of the materials, the texture and hue of the finishes, as well as the experience the pieces have acquired during their lifespan. It feels like a shop full of characters, each one of them telling you their life story over a game of boules and a glass of rosé.

covet:
farmhouse linen tablecloths
french painted armoirs
antique bilboquets (ball & pin game)
vintage tinware
vintage glassware
farmhouse confit jars
mühldorfer bedding
neom candles

present

wearable menswear and great coffee, to boot

140 shoreditch high street e1 6je. between french and rivington
tube: liverpool street / old street or overground: shoreditch high street
020.7033.0500 www.present-london.com
mon - fri 10.30a - 7p sat 11a - 6:30p sun noon - 5p

opened in 2009. owners: eddie prendergast and steve davies
all major credit cards accepted
online shopping

shoreditch > **s25**

There's a very accomplished team behind *Present*, and you can feel it as soon as you walk in the door. They know their menswear, all right. They also know what makes customers tick. The first thing that greets you is the La Victoria Arduino coffee machine operated by Gwilym, the world's (nicest) barista champion. Yes, you are going to have a good time here at *Present* and you may well emerge with a new treasured favourite piece of clothing, if you're a boy. If you are, like me, a non boy, don't worry, there's plenty at *Present* to tempt you too—starting with a demon flat white.

covet:
present label clothing
der sammler solo
trickers of northampton shoes
nom de guerre trousers
winga and horns
nigel cabourn
postler ferguson paper guns
cire trudon candles

retrouvius

reclamation and design

2a ravensworth road nw10 5nr. entrance on harrow road. tube: kensal green
020.8960.6060 www.retrouvius.com
mon - sat 10a - 6p

opened in 2005. owners: adam hills and maria speake
visa. mc
online shopping. custom design

kensal green > 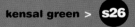 s26

Retrouvius is salvage with a twist, where the original form is honored, but the function gets modernized. Example: what would you do if you came across a shedload of interesting glass funnels? At *Retrouvius* they might source cloth-covered wiring and lamp fittings and then, presto chango!: gorgeous hanging lamps. This is style magic at work, the proverbial rabbit pulled out of the hat. Most pieces though will need no fairy dust sprinkled on them to imagine them in your possibly somewhat larger and emptier home.

covet:
enamel lampshades
hardwood worktops
matlock stone flooring tables
cast iron ex-patent office adjustable shelving
reclaimed architrave mirrors
school chairs
metal screens
fireplaces

ryantown

papercut art fun

126 columbia road e2 7rg. between ezra and ravenscroft
tube: liverpool street / old street or overground: shoreditch high street
020.7613.1510 www.misterrob.co.uk
sat noon - 5p sun 9a - 4p

opened in 2008. owner: robert ryan
visa. mc
online shopping. commissioned work

shoreditch >  **s27**

Every street should have a *Ryantown* on it, dispensing whimsical creativity, tickling imaginations and reawakening the inner child of everyone who walks past. Rob's talent is at once prodigious, precocious and prolific, so you'll find all sorts of collaborations and interesting practical things in *Ryantown*. Last time I was in, I bought a skirt kit which is impractical in the extreme, given my lamentable sewing skill level. But I will conquer the needle and thread because I want to wear some *Ryantown* whimsy. I will look down at my skirt and feel happy, I know it. *Ryantown* forever.

covet:
ryantown:
   screenprint pictures
   papercut pictures
   cushions kit
   ceramic printed tiles
   wall measuring chart
   acrylic & wooden keys
   cards

scp

a veritable smorgasbord of great design

135 - 137 curtain road ec2a 3bx. between rivington and old streets
tube: liverpool street / old street or overground: shoreditch high street
020.7739.1869 www.scp.co.uk
mon - sat 9.30a - 6p sun 11a - 5p

opened in 1985. owner: sheridan coakley
visa. mc
online shopping. registries. custom orders

shoreditch > **s28**

SCP is the big daddy of London design shops. It manages to keep its nose ahead of the competition with house-brand furniture that beautifully compliments the classic designs to be found here, and also through the eagle eyes of its buyers, who always seem to find the hot new quirk before anyone else. My current loves on offer are the bird tables (which hang, of course—this is *SCP* after all) and a classic Yngve Ekström chair, but I reserve the right to shift my affections next time I visit to see what catches my fancy.

covet:
matthew hilton for scp oscar armchair
thomas heatherwick spun stool
modernica charles eames rocker
burleigh ironstone jug
opinel knife
anne black ceramic jewellery
gavin christman birdball feeder
donna wilson nos da cushions

silverprint

the ultimate photographic printing shop
12 valentine place se1 8qh. between webber and blackfriars
tube: southwark or waterloo
020.7620.0844 www.silverprint.co.uk
mon - fri 9.30a - 5.30p sat 10a - 1p

opened in 1984. owner: martin reed
visa. mc
online shopping. darkroom services. gallery

waterloo > **s29**

The alchemy of the printing process is my favourite part of photography, albeit one that I don't get to do often enough. Photographers of my acquaintance with darkrooms, rather than laptops and software, are always bemoaning the loss of a favourite paper, or a much loved thingumajig, integral to the dark art of the printing process. They do all rave about *Silverprint*, however, as the one place you are sure to find these items, if still manufactured, and used to print photographic images. I think this is a classic case of use it or lose it. Now, where's my film camera?

covet:
portfolio boxes
foma paper
darkroom equipment
specialist books
pinhole cameras
refurbed & recovered olympus tripods
digital inks & papers
kentmere bromide paper

social suicide

twisted ivy league fashion for men
20 7617 7696 www.socialsuicide.co.uk
see website for "gypsy lease" locations

opened in 2009. owners: matthew grey and simon waterfall
visa. mc
custom modifications

no storefront >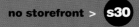

Social Suicide is all about serious tailoring done with a raised eyebrow. Take for example the holidaze summer jacket: its lining is printed with board games you can play using the change in your pockets and it also has a deep pocket lined with polishing cloth for your shades. I spent ages in here taking pictures, partly because the banter was top class and partly because I kept sneakily trying on the jackets. I couldn't resist. Matthew admitted that one of them would look pretty cool on me with a couple of minor, girl, alterations. Womenswear next please…?

A dozen uncompromising, single-minded, passionate, visionary & utterly inspiring suits...

covet:
social suicide:
  holidaze jackets
  winston churchill single-breasted,
    3-piece, pinstripe flannel suit
  cotton, twisted seam summer trousers
  braces
  sunglasses
trousers london jeans

soler

vivacious women's clothing
88 bevington road w10 5tw. between golborne and raddington
tube: ladbroke grove
020.8968.4694 www.solerdesigns.co.uk
tue - fri 10a - 6p sat noon - 6p or by appointment

opened in 2010. owner: alex subidé soler
visa. mc
custom orders. bespoke services

portobello > s31

Soler is a ray of sunshine in the sometimes drab landscape of chic. It's a tonic to be surrounded by Alex's (the Spanish ex-model turned designer) riot of colour and diaphanous one-off fabrics. And whereas the thought "this design would be perfect if only it was in that fabric and in my size" usually signals the end of the shopping trip, in *Soler* it's only the beginning as they will make up any of Alex's designs in any fabric, in your size. Oh yes, it's true. So now you see why the moment I'm done writing this book, I'm treating myself to an afternoon at *Soler*.

covet:
soler:
  diaphenous jumpsuits
  dresses
  skirts
  shirts
  short run fabrics
silk fabrics hand painted by alex's sister,
  monica, an oil painter

susannah hunter

leather handbags and furnishings
7 rugby street wc1n 3qt. between lamb's conduit and millman. tube: holborn
020.7692.3798 www.susannahhunter.com
mon - fri 10a - 6p

opened in 2007. owner: susannah hunter
all major credit cards accepted
online shopping. commissions

holborn > **s32**

I love a place that does just one thing to perfection, especially when the thing includes handbags and other little bags to go into handbags. *Susannah Hunter* and her team of nimble-fingered seamstresses adorn not only leather bags of distinction, but also furniture and stunning room screens with leather flowers, delicate or blowsy to suit every mood. Unlike the Connaught Street location, here you can hear the workshop, in the back part of the shop, making their gardens out of leather. Come to *Susannah Hunter* and feel, for a moment, how a bee must feel, in a summer garden, if that bee loves handbags like I do.

169

tatty devine

cheeky jewellery

44 monmouth street wc2h 9ep. earlham street and tower street
tube: covent garden or leicester square
020.7836.2685 www.tattydevine.com
mon - sat 11a - 7p sun noon - 5p

opened in 2009. owners: rosie wolfenden and harriet vine
all major credit cards accepted
online shopping. custom orders

covent garden > **s33**

Tatty Devine is such a London thing. In fact, for me it's even more parochial than that: it's an East London thing. I saw *Tatty Devine* start up in Brick Lane a few years ago and I have watched them getting it together, gaining a buzz internationally and opening this, their second shop—all without losing the exuberant spirit of fun that propelled them in the first place. So step into this Covent Garden funhouse and soak up that East London vibe. Free yourself for a moment from the shackles of bland bourgeois jewellery and say hello to the fearlessly flamboyant *Tatty Devine* style.

covet:
tatty devine:
   acrylic & wood cutout necklaces
   telephone brooches
   anchor earrings
antoni & alison
peter jensen
eley kishimoto
minimarket

tenderproduct

design shop full of quirky things
6 cecil court wc2n 4he. between charing cross and st martin's
tube: leicester square
020.7379.9464 www.tenderproduct.com
tue - sat 10a - 6p

opened in 2009. owner: etan ilfeld
all major credit cards accepted
online shopping. workshops for young designers. gallery

covent garden > s34

I almost don't want to put *Tenderproduct* in this book, even though I know that I must. I want the shop to flourish, because it's great, and I want you all to know about it and all the lovely work in here by talented under the radar designers who deserve attention. But I do wish that my friends wouldn't have to read about it because now my cover will be blown, and everyone will know where their birthday presents have been coming from this year and, well, then I too will get presents from here, and... oh, everything will be fine. *Tenderproduct* everybody! *Tenderproduct!*

covet:
diy design it yourself deck
silver tape timer
holy toast miracle bread stamper
stuart gardiner seasonal vegetable tea towels
gary welch stereoscopic viewers
jill green hand sewn silk screened purses
jang-oh hong coloured pencil key ring
mouche solar-powered fly robot

the button queue

buttons galore

76 marylebone lane w1u 2pr. between wigmore and hinde. tube: bond street
020.7935.1505 www.thebuttonqueen.co.uk
mon - fri 10a - 5p sat 10a - 2p

opened in 1960. owners: martyn and isabel frith
visa. mc
online shopping

marylebone > 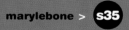 **s35**

While I was in *The Button Queen*, a lady came in and began describing the button she needed. Another customer then came in and asked a different staff member for a button for a dinner jacket and was out of the shop in thirty seconds flat, button in hand. Some time later the first lady had, surprisingly, still not found her button and had to leave. Undaunted, the staffer suggested she send a sample of the dress material in the post so the search could continue. That level of care, whether you are a fashion student, a lawyer in a hurry or an elderly lady with a train to catch, is what I love about *The Button Queen*.

covet:
buttons of every conceivable size, shape, vintage, material & provenance:
   italian glass buttons
   wedgewood buttons
   18th century french enamelled buttons
   modern plastic buttons
   buttons in horn
cufflinks & dress shirt studs

the convenience store

fashion without seasons

1a hazlewood tower w10 5dt. where hazlewood road and golborne gardens meet
tube: ladbroke grove
020.8968.9095 www.theconveniencestorefashion.co.uk
fri - sat 11a - 6p or by appointment

opened in 2008. owner: andrew ibi
all major credit cards accepted
online shopping

portobello >  **s36**

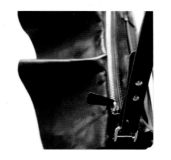

There is something wonderful about *The Convenience Store*. This shop sits at the bottom of a tower block, opposite the iconic Trellick Towers, for all the world like a dry cleaners or a corner shop. But inside you'll find an avant garde world of clothing where the seasonality of fashion is not the dominating story. instead Andrew sells pieces he likes whether they be spring or fall, and talks about the clothing's character like it's a close friend. Once you have your fill of contemporary fashion, you can wander across to the lovely *Rellick* for some vintage accessories to complete your look.

covet:
camilla skovgaard
boudicca
hussein chalayan
richard sorger
superfertile jewellery
michael lewis shoes
erika trotzig
af vandervorst

177

the last tuesday society

tongue-in-cheek cabinet of curiosities

11 mare street e8 8rp. corner of andrew's road
tube: bethnal green or rail: cambridge heath
020.7998.3617 www.thelasttuesdaysociety.org
wed - sun noon - 7p or by appointment

opened in 2009. owners: suzette field and viktor wynd
all major credit cards accepted
events. prop hire. gallery

london fields > s37

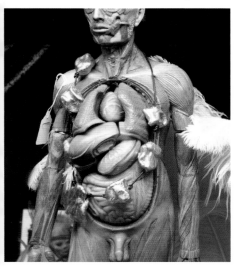

A young woman came into the extraordinary Kunstkamera of a shop-come-gallery, *The Last Tuesday Society*, while I was there and asked "Do you have an arm, like a baby's arm, maybe made of porcelain?" Her utter disbelief that they did not have said arm was a sight to behold, but she left later, laden with other curios, completely happy. Shop, gallery and micro-museum, here you will find originals and theatrical fakery, admired equally for their bravado and goosebumpery. Here too you may attend events and talks on weird and wonderful subjects, all given with a twinkle in the eye.

covet:
two-headed teddy bears
taxidermy
masks
curious confectioners my little edible pony
gold pig snout
muskrat skulls
mounted butterflies
feather brooches

the powder room

retro style beauty makeovers
136 columbia road e2 7rg. opposite ezra street
tube: liverpool street / old street or overground: shoreditch high street
020.7729.1365 www.thepowderpuffgirls.com
sat noon - 6p sun 10a - 4p or by appointment

opened in 2009. owner: katie reynolds
visa. mc
online shopping. beauty services. wedding makeup. classes

shoreditch > s38

It's an odd juxtaposition on a Sunday morning: the flower market outside, with cries of "two bunches for ten" and *The Powder Room,* with its subdued hubbub of buffing, as the Powder Puff Girls work their prettifying magic on women who drink tea and revel in the gentle femininity of it all. I haven't been for a retro makeover here yet, but it's on my list, though I think I will come in on a Saturday. Then I can enjoy the fruits of their labours all Saturday evening, rather than try to improve my Sunday 'day after' appearance, when I fear their ministrations might be wasted.

covet:
powderpuff girls:
  shimmer powderpuff
  hair, nails and makeup services
blouse and skirt cosmetics
diane brill eyeshadow
paul & jo lip gloss
mavala nail colours
japonesque lash kit

tim bryars ltd

antiquarian maps, rare books and prints
8 cecil court wc2n 4he. between charing cross road and st martin's lane
tube: leicester square
020.7836.1910 www.paralos.co.uk
mon - fri 11a - 6p sat noon - 5p

opened in 2004. owner: tim bryars
all major credit cards accepted
online shopping. international shipping

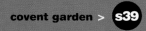

covent garden > s39

I came into *Tim Bryars*' shop a few years ago with an innocent question about an old map of London. I emerged, dazzled by this magical world of cartography. Tim is an expert, so in love with his subject, and with such wit, that I was entranced as I learned how early maps were as much about power as geography. For example, the fact that the cartographer of the interregnum map drew all the trees in St James' Park, when in fact they had been felled by anti-royalists, makes his map a powerful political statement, in favor of the monarchy, of course. Tim should teach history. Well, in a gloriously accessible way, he does.

covet:
17th century:
  jan cloppenburgh edition of
    mercator map of europe
  justus danckerts map of the globe
  1610 edition of quintillian with notes in latin
20th century:
  1935 edward camy's a good natured map
    of alaska

tracey neuls

beautifully crafted shoes for women
29 marylebone lane w1u 2nq. corner of hinde mews. tube: bond street
020.7935.0039 www.tn29.com
mon - fri 11a - 6.30p sat - sun noon - 5p

opened in 2006. owner: tracey neuls
all major credit cards accepted
custom orders

marylebone >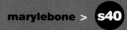

Tracey Neuls' shop is a shoe lover's paradise, filled with beautiful workmanship and great design all presented with theatrical flair. Each shoe here takes you off into a different realm of fashion and footwear synthesis, crying out to marry itself to favourite pieces of clothing in your wardrobe. Now at last I understand the look that a woman will give you when you compliment her on her *Tracey Neul* shoes. It's the complicit glance that identifies you as someone who recognizes how special these shoes are and that those who wear them are a breed apart.

covet:
tracey neuls:
  limited edition fa105
  tnb10
  tn _ 29 vf110
  tn _ 29 jb105
custom sizes for odd sized feet
custom wedding shoes
nina saunders' bronze cast pea necklace

wingate studio=shop

talented young printmaker's studio shop
144 columbia road e2 7rg. opposite ezra street
tube: liverpool street / old street or overground: shoreditch high street
07786.320480 www.wingateprint.com
sat noon - 5p sun 9a - 3p or by appointment

opened in 2010. owner: sam wingate
visa. mc
online shopping. classes. custom designs / commissions

shoreditch >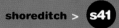

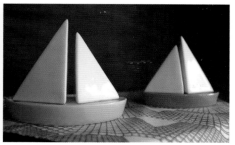

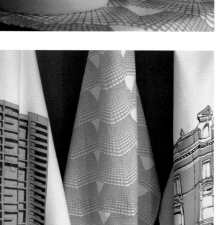

Some shops look great to the eye, but even better through the lens. And so it is with *Wingate Studio = Shop* which I liked immediately but fell for hook, line and sinker while curing the taking of these pictures. Sam's urban screenprints deserve close inspection, with every tower block and pub building imbued with sullen beauty. He sells some lovely creations by friends as well, including the wondrously calming Takae Mizutani "memory of Falmouth" ceramic boats, which instantly whisk you out of the urban landscape to the seaside. Climb the narrow staircase up to *Wingate Studio = Shop* and enjoy.

covet:
wingate:
  cushions
  tea towels
  sweats
  aprons
  wallpaper commissions
sarah palmer sketch books
me me me bottle vases

w.sitch & company ltd

antique light fittings

48 berwick street w1f 8jd. between noel and oxford. tube: oxford circus
020.7437.3776 www.wsitch.co.uk
mon - fri 8:30a - 5p sat 9.30a - 1p

opened in 1776. owners: messrs. ronald, james and laurence sitch
cash only
online shopping. custom orders

soho >

I must have walked past the door to *W.Sitch & Company* a thousand times without ever knowing what was inside. If I think about this five storey house filled with mostly brass antique lamps for long, I get goosebumps—I feel them coming on now. If you've read any of the Harry Potter books, think Diagon Alley and shopping for a wand. Imagine a similiar world when you enter here looking for an antique brass lamp, and upon wandering around, the lamp you should own will light up, suddenly. *W.Sitch* is a wonderful, hidden treasure, and I highly recommend it to all.

covet:
brass wall sconces
table lamps
candleabra
lanterns
chandeliers
electroliers
floor standards
glass bowls for lamps

yvonne damant

women's designer clothing
13 richmond hill tw10 6re. opposite lancaster mews
tube, overground or rail: richmond
020.8940.0514 www.yvonnedamant.com
wed - sat 10.30a - 5.30p

opened in 1981. owner: yvonne damant
all major credit cards accepted
custom orders

richmond > 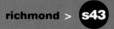 **s43**

Yvonne Damant is a chic womenswear designer who must surely sell her clothes to the rock star wives who live on Richmond Hill. Her clothes are great, edgy yet assured, and I thank Vanessa who works at *Petersham Nurseries* whose tip lead me here. My prescription for an ideal day would be lunch at *Petersham*, then a stroll to walk off your feast, pausing at the top of the hill to take in what is the most spectacular, breathtaking view of the curve in the Thames into London I have ever seen. Then head down the hill to Yvonne's shop to take in her lovely view of fashion.

covet:
yvonne damant
ann demeulemeester
rick owens
share spirit
biya
peachoo + krejberg
rundholz
l'autre chose shoes

etc.

the eat.shop guides were created by kaie wellman and are published by cabazon books

eat.shop london 2nd edition was written, researched and photographed by caroline loncq

editing: kaie wellman   copy editing and fact checking: eve connell
map and layout production: julia dickey and bryan wolf

caroline: once you author an *eat.shop guide*, your antennae are out and you become an irritating companion—constantly craning your neck to catch the name of a tantalising shop or trying to find out where that delicious smell is wafting from. i must thank my foodie friends for their suggestions: al, rosie, matty, oz, tom, daisy, joel, sarah, lou, the league of fatties, affy and adam. also my fashionista friends, tina and jo and rod, plus all the shop and restaurant owners who helped so much. lastly my thanks go to my family—simon, jonjo and my mum susie, for understanding why i disappeared with my camera and bicycle for so long.

cabazon books: eat.shop london 2nd edition
ISBN-13 9780982325490

the *eat.shop guides* are distributed by independent publishers group in the u.s.: www.ipgbook.com
and in the united kingdom by portfolio books: www.portfoliobooks.com

to peer further into the world of *eat.shop* and to buy books, please visit: www.eatshopguides.com